They Led The Way

The Story Of Pathfinder Squadron 156

by

Michael Philip Wadsworth

Highgate Publications (Beverley) Ltd.
1992

British Library Cataloguing in Publication Data

Wadsworth, Michael Philip
    They Led the Way : Story of Pathfinder Squadron 156
    I. Title
    940.54

ISBN 0-948929-58-8

Cover Pictures;

Top right: *W/C 'Tiny' Ison , D.S.O., D.F.C.. (eighth from left), C.O. of 156 Squadron*
                 in 1945 with aircrew and ground crew.
Middle left: *Three Lancasters of 156 Squadron in flight.*
Bottom right: *G/C R. W. P. Collings, D.F.C., A.F.C. (centre), C.O. of 156 Squadron from*
                 June, 1943, to January, 1944, with the Officers before a briefing.

© Michael Philip Wadsworth, 1992

ISBN 0 948929 58 8

Published by Highgate Publications (Beverley) Ltd.
24 Wylies Road, Beverley, HU17 7AP.
Telephone (0482) 866826

Printed and Typeset in 10 on 11pt Times by
Colourspec, Unit 7, Tokenspire Park,
Hull Road, Woodmansey, Beverley. HU17 0TB.
Telephone (0482) 864264

CONTENTS

THEY LED THE WAY

THE STORY OF 156 PATHFINDER SQUADRON

Chapter   *Page*

DEDICATION

To my father:
F/O Philip Wadsworth (156 Squadron),
Who failed to return on the night of April 27/28th 1944, and all those who made the one-way journey

and

To my mother:
Margaret Wadsworth,
Without whose help this book would not have been written, and to all the air crew widows.

ACKNOWLEDGEMENTS

I am grateful to the following for their help in the writing of this book, and for their encouragement and inspiration:

Mrs. Ly Bennett, who said of my intended project, 'Do it now', her late husband, A/V/M. Bennett's advice on most courses of action;

A. W. Black, for his excellently produced video recordings of Pathfinder reunions at Warboys;

Nigel Brass;

Ron Breeze, who lent to me a log book and a lengthy diary;

Peter Coggan;

Charles Dee, who presented me with a preaching scarf embroidered with Pathfinder insignia, on behalf of the 156 Squadron Memorial Association;

Bob Edmonds;

Paul Freeman of HMSO for the loan of the Official History;

Alf French;

Arthur Fry;

Sam Hall, who supplied me with much information and encouragement, and who lent me a copy of his unpublished memoirs, *Time Flying*;

Harold Hernaman;

Mrs. Eileen Hodgson, my aunt, for much support at the crucial periods;

Jimmy and Olivia Hughes;

Taff and Norah Jones, who helped to start all of this and who gave me permission to use some photographs in this publication from their excellent personal collection;

Paddy McCrum;

Rab MacKenzie;

John Markham, Martyn and Irene Kirby, and Barry Sage of Highgate Publications for patient and courteous advice and co-operation;

Miss Grace Moore, who has told me much about life in Warboys, when 156 Squadron operated from the airfield;

John Needham;

Douglas Radcliffe of the R.A.F. Museum, Hendon;

Mrs Margaret Spirit;

Bob Trotter, who compiled the 156 Squadron Register;

Mrs Shelia Redshaw for her patience, skill, and flexibility with a word processor;

Bernard Warren;

Mrs Margaret Wadsworth, my mother whose major contribution to this book is reflected in the dedication;

Mrs. Tamara Wadsworth, my wife, who gave me space, time, support and encouragement during the writing of this book;

The staff of the County Record Office in Cambridge and Michael Farrar, the County Archivist;

The staff of the County Record Office in Huntingdon;

Members of the Pathfinder Association, and of the 156 Squadron Association.

The poem at the end of the eighth chapter is by John Pudney, and taken from *Ten Summers: Poems 1933-1943* (Bodley Head, 1944) p. 48. It is called 'Security'.

ABBREVIATIONS.

A.F.C.	Air Force Cross.
AOC	Air Officer Commanding.
AI	Airborn Interception.
A/M	Air Marshal.
A/P	Aiming Point.
ASI	Airspeed Indicator.
A/V/M	Air Vice-Marshal
CAS	Chief of Air staff.
C. in C.	Commander in Chief.
CGM	Conspicuous Gallantry Medal.
C.O	Commanding Officer.
Cpl.	Corporal.
D.F.C.	Distinguished Flying Cross.
D.F.M.	Distinguished Flying Medal.
D.S.O.	Distinguished Service Order.
ETA	Estimated Time of Arrival.
F/L	Flight Lieutenant.
F/O	Flying Officer.
F/S	Flight Sergeant.
G/C	Group Captain.
HCU	Heavy Conversion Unit.
H2S	A radar aid towards identifying the target (said to come from an earlier code, 'Home Sweet Home', though this is disputed).
HQ	Headquarters.
JU	Junkers (German aircraft, as in JU88)
L.A.C.	Leading Aircraftsman
LNSF	Light Night Striking Force (a force of Pathfinder Mosquito squadrons).
ME	Messerschmitt (as in ME109, ME110, etc).
Met.	Meteorological (Aircrew referred to 'Met.' as the weather report, or as those who made these reports).
Op(s)	Operation(s)

ORB	Operations Record Book.
OTU	Operational Training Unit.
PFF	Pathfinder Force.
P/O	Pilot Officer.
P.O.W.	Prisoner of War.
R.A.A.F.	Royal Australian Air Force.
R.A.F.	Royal Air Force.
R.C.A.F.	Royal Canadian Air Force.
R.N.Z.A.F.	Royal New Zealand Air Force.
RT	Radio Transmitter/Transmission.
S.A.A.F.	South African Air Force.
Sgt.	Sergeant.
S/L	Squadron Leader.
T.I	Target Indicator.
U.S.A.F.	United States Air Force (as it is now called).
U.S.A.A.F.	United States Army Air Force. (wartime designation).
V.C.	Victoria Cross.
W.A.A.F.	Women's Auxiliary Air Force.
W/C	Wing Commander.
W/O	Warrant Officer.

CHAPTER 1

IN SEARCH OF A FLIGHT-ENGINEER

'Look to the rock from which you were hewn, and to the quarry from which you were digged. Look to Abraham your father, and to Sarah who bore you.'

(Isaiah 51: 1-2)

Many books begin with an interior voice. Mine kept on saying, 'Search and write.' The search was for the man who was my father, less than twice my age. The writing is what you are now reading. It chronicles the life of an R.A.F Squadron, 156 Squadron, one of the famous Pathfinder Squadrons, who, as this book's title suggests, led the way for the main force of Bomber Command. They marked the route, found the way to distant, heavily defended targets, illuminated the target for the following bombers, and, all too often, did not get back. My father, Philip Wadsworth, ended his life on 156 Squadron, flying as flight engineer in a Lancaster piloted by the C.O., W/C Eaton, on the night of April 27/28th, 1944. The aircraft was one of eighteen shot down over Friedrichshafen in southern Germany. None survived from my father's aircraft. He had started life in aircrew as a flight engineer in a main force squadron in 1 Group in September 1942. 1 Group was based in Lincolnshire, and 103 Squadron was based at Elsham Wolds, on a windy escarpment just south of the Humber, where, at present, the Humber Bridge's southern approach begins. A two-year apprenticeship at Halton, and a course at St. Athan had prepared him for that first operational flight to Duisburg on September 7th, 1942, as flight engineer in Halifax W1189, captained by a Canadian pilot, F/S 'Roley' Newitt. His operational life at Elsham Wolds spanned the time chronicled in that classic of Bomber Command literature, *No Moon Tonight*, written by an Australian navigator, Don Charlwood. By January 30th 1943 F/S Wadsworth had completed eighteen 'ops' with the same crew. At that stage, due to the severity of casualties, no one in 103 had completed the standard number of operations in a tour, thirty. He and his crew, and three other crews, high on the operational ladder were then 'screened', and taken off 'ops'. The nearby Heavy Conversion

Unit at Blyton, No. 1662, needed instructors on Lancasters, 103 Squadron had converted to Lancasters in the previous November, and so the three senior crews at Elsham were posted there.

Don Charlwood's narrative chronicles the life of the squadron in late 1942 and early 1943, the roll call of the missing, as they took off in their Halifaxes or Lancasters into the dark nights, and made their way over the North Sea, and sombre reflections in and among and between the nights out in Scunthorpe at the celebrated 'Oswald'. My mother, who lived on the other side of the Humber, in Driffield, East Yorkshire, not far from Bridlington, used to catch the ferry over the Humber at weekends during this Elsham period and stay at the village of Barnetby near the airfield. The little boy of the house where she stayed used to tell her how he'd seen the aircraft being bombed up that afternoon so it was 'ops on' for that night. It was a not untypical life for an aircrew wife. Quite often the entire crew took her out with them. Roley Newitt, tall and fair haired, was a good pilot, close to his crew and they to him. He survived the war and returned to Canada as S/L R. M. Newitt, D.F.C. and Bar, and still resides in Vancouver.

Many pilots and aircrew from 103 Squadron were posted to 156 Squadron to which my father was posted in January 1944. Notable among the pilots were S/L 'Syd' Cook, D.F.C., D.F.M., who went missing in October, 1943, and SL R.F. Griffin, D.S.O., D.F.C., who survived the war and became a civil airline pilot.

For an airminded youth like Philip Wadsworth to join the R.A.F. and gain an apprenticeship at Halton was the fulfilment of boyhood dreams. Like my mother he was born and brought up in the little East Yorkshire market town of Driffield, attended Driffield Church of England Junior School, where his father was a teacher (while his mother taught in the Infants School next door), and went to the ancient Grammar School in Bridlington, leaving the school for Halton in Buckinghamshire, for training as an R.A.F. apprentice in 1937. He was one of four children, with a sister and two brothers, and his twin ambitions were to play the organ and join the R.A.F. He succeeded, during his short life, in doing both. His father taught him how to play the organ, and he became a gifted organist, much in demand to play the instrument in local churches, though he had a like passion for cinema organs, and used to be allowed to play mighty Wurlitzers, whenever this was possible, and where compliant cinema organists were willing. He had seven years in the R.A.F., from the start of his entry into Halton at sixteen in 1937 to his death over Friedtichshafen at twenty-two in 1944.

My father's other ambition, every bit as driving as the other two, was to marry my mother, a childhood sweetheart, which he did on September 12th 1942. The special licence had been arranged, the wedding dresses made, a telephone call made from Elsham to say that Saturday 12th was to be the date. On the night of the 10th, however, he had another 'op' to do before leave. Over Dusseldorf the wedding plans almost came to nothing, as his Halifax nearly collided with a JU88 over the target, and the flak was heavy among the 300 searchlights.

When he was married on the Saturday at All Saints' Church in Driffield, one of his fingers, which had been grazed by a flak splinter, was bound up. Since that telephone call on the Thursday, not mentioning the 'op' still to be done, arrangements were set in motion, and after the wedding a reception was held for 130 guests at the Masonic Hall in Driffield.

Driffield, this little Yorkshire Market town, was destined to be my home. When my father died I was ten months old, and so never knew him, growing up with mother and grandparents. Like a larger version of Warboys, wartime Driffield was an aircrew centre. The nearby pre-war R.A.F. Station housed a series of bomber squadrons in 4 Group from the first day of the war and onwards. The Driffield Squadrons included some famous ones, 77 in which that celebrated Pathfinder, C.O. of 7 Squadron at Oakington and later the N.T.U. at Warboys, G/C 'Hamish' Mahaddie, D.S.O., D.F.C., A.F.C., Czech M.C., began his first tour as a sergeant pilot, and 102, in which a young pilot officer, Leonard Cheshire, made his first operational flight, both of them in Whitleys. At a later time Driffield housed the Canadian Squadron 405, which later still became a Pathfinder Squadron, based at Bourn in Cambridgeshire, and in the later part of 1944 two Australian Squadrons, 462 and 466. So 'the Capital of the Yorkshire Wolds' played generous host to these diverse nationalities, and aircrew made the most of their stand downs among the town's hostelries, so much so that the celebrated Buck Hotel in Middle Street was dubbed 'Hangar Number Six'.

After early schooling in this town of aircrew associations I went to Pocklington, fifteen miles away, for my secondary education. During the war Pocklington had outside of it yet another 4 Group aerodrome, and I recall drilling with the school Combined Cadet Force on the old abandoned airfield, from where the Halifaxes took off for Germany. The squadron based at Pocklington was 102 Squadron, which had moved there from Driffield, and it had the unhappy distinction of suffering the third highest overall casualties in Bomber Command. In January 1944, during the Battle of Berlin, there were two nights when the squadron from Pocklington lost nine aircraft in all. As a schoolboy the area was alive with stories of a war that ended ten years before, of returning Halifaxes crashing in the old canal, of the school being raked by the cannon fire of a JU88 one night, who mistook the school buildings for the aerodrome, of a heavy preponderance of Canadians who were, of course, very popular with the local girls. A thriller writer, Spencer Dunmore, now living in Canada, has written a novel about aircrew at Pocklington, entitled *Bomb Run*, published in 1971. The town is thinly disguised as 'Brocklington', by a kind of novelist's Grimm's Law, but the description of language and location, the proximity of school and airfield call out for this identification.

After university at Oxford, and theological training, I was ordained deacon at York Minster in 1970, and priest in 1971. During my years of ordained ministry I worked in northern urban parishes, with a spell as a Cambridge college chaplain in between. And so, in November, 1989, I came to be Vicar of Haddenham and Wilburton, two villages in the old Isle of Ely, in the Cambridgeshire fens, twelve miles away from Warboys. From an upstairs window you can see the old bomber airfield at Witchford, home of 115 Squadron, while, in another direction, the splendid tower of St. Andrew's church, Sutton, can be seen, quite near to Mepal airfield, where the New Zealanders of 75 Squadron were based. I had not been long in my new parish, when, during a Remembrance Sunday service at St. Peter's, Wilburton, I preached about my background and my father's short time and death on 156 Squadron. After the service the server, Thomas Robinson, introduced me to his family, his mother Mrs. 'Wiggy' Robinson, a parishioner and resident in the village, and his grandparents. These were 'Taff' and Norah Jones. Both had the deepest and most lasting association with Warboys and 156 Squadron. Both, in fact, met on the squadron, have lived in Warboys ever since, and live there now. Taff worked as ground crew in 156 Squadron, servicing aircraft in 'B' flight from the formation of the squadron at Warboys (indeed he was at Alconbury before that time) and at Upwood. Norah, (nee Shephard) was during wartime manageress of the N.A.A.F.I. on the W.A.A.F. site on the airfield. Taff is now Secretary of the 156 Squadron Association, and this chance meeting had a number of consequences, an invitation to preach at the annual Pathfinder service at Warboys in May at St. Mary Magdalene, which has been repeated on two further occasions, visits to the home of Taff and Norah and, with that, a privileged glimpse of old photographs and a host of memorabilia, and meetings with 156 veterans who have given me much information and inspiration. Last May (1991) a window to the Pathfinders was dedicated in St. Mary Magdalene, a simple and beautiful memorial to those who flew in their Wellingtons and Lancasters over this ancient church from the nearby airfield and failed to return, and August, 1992, the fiftieth anniversary of the formation of the Pathfinder force, sees the dedication of plaques at Warboys and Upwood on Monday August 17th, after a special service in Ely Cathedral on Sunday August 16th. And so, against the background of all this remembering, and in an effort to dig down to my own roots and origins, I offer to all who may be interested what I have found about one of the earliest operational Pathfinder Squadrons, 156, in which many, many young men lived, served, and died. For these are the things I discovered when I went in search of a flight-engineer.

156 Squadron in May, 1943, taken at Warboys, with W/C Rivett-Carnac as C.O.

(*Taff Jones*)

CHAPTER 2

'OPS IN A WIMPY'
PATHFINDER WELLINGTONS

'Ops in a Wimpy, ops in a Wimpy,
Who'll come on ops in a Wimpy with me?
And I sang as the ack-ack worked so patiently,
Who'll come on ops in a Wimpy with me?'

Popular aircrew song.
(To tune of *Waltzing Matilda*).

It was a strange way to start a group which led the way and guided the greatest aerial armada in history. The C. in C., Sir Arthur Harris approached W/C Donald Bennett early in July, 1942, and his appointment as Commander of the Pathfinder force was confirmed on July 13th. Only a month later four squadrons in East Anglia and the East Midlands were in place, and a day later they went to war. There were no special navigational aids or target finding or marking facilities. The radio navigational aid known as Gee, which employed three ground stations to provide a navigator with a fix, decreased in accuracy the further the bomber crews went, and was vulnerable to jamming. So the old 'Goon Box', as it was called, was of little use in the face of such problems. The C. in C. let it be known he did not agree with such a force. Special squadrons smacked too much of elitism. The winnowing out of tried and proven crews would lower morale and fatally weaken mainline squadrons at a time when the loss rate was improving upon the absolute nadir of fortunes of late 1941, but which had still a long way to go, if a greater and ever increasing tonnage of bombs were ever to be delivered upon particular targets, accurately found, and with aiming points marked.

Some advocates of a target finding force argued that special squadrons were the only solution and others that every squadron should have its own marker crews. In the end Marshal of the Royal Air Force, Sir Charles Portal, and Mr Winston Churchill were in accord on the matter: special squadrons would be formed. Yet again the 'how' factor was not tackled. That was left to the new commander, the recently appointed G/C Donald Bennett (so recently a Wing

Commander) to provide for, in negotiation with the C. in C. Thus every group provided a squadron to make up this controversial new force, and it was left to G/C Bennett to choose the aerodromes. The Pathfinders, therefore, began with five squadrons, provided by group commanders sometimes willingly, and mostly reluctantly, as follows below.

From 3 Group came No. 7 Squadron with Stirlings. They were stationed at a solid pre-war station at Oakington near Cambridge. From 5 Group came No. 83 Squadron, to be stationed at Wyton, where the best weather reports were available, and the site of G/C Bennett's headquarters. They were fortunate enough to have Lancasters right from the start. Also at Wyton were pressurised Wellingtons, to be devoted to testing, developing and using the new navigational device code-named 'Oboe', formed into 109 Squadron and taken out of the Wireless Intelligence Development Unit of No. 2 Group. Oboe was a radar device for blind bombing, far more sophisticated than Gee. The musical code name derived from a radio pulse which produced a note in the pilot's headphones. Ultimately Mosquitoes were fitted with Oboe. They could go up higher than other aircraft, and so operate their device at a greater range, unaffected by the curvature of the earth, which interfered with the signals which came from ground stations in England.

To Oakington and Wyton the new commander attached two satellites, Graveley and Warboys, both of them, like Wyton, close to Huntingdon, but which bore all the characteristics of hostilities only stations, and which inevitably, in the best prophetic tradition, have now gone under the plough. Graveley housed 35 Squadron from 4 Group, which was, after all, G/C Bennett's former group (he had previously been C.O. of 10 and 77 Squadrons), and was equipped with Halifaxes. That left Warboys, which accommodated 156 Squadron, from 1 Group, the subject of this memoir, which was equipped with Wellingtons, nicknamed 'Wimpys', after the popular cartoon character J. Wellington Wimpy, who had an inordinate passion for consuming hamburgers. The motto of 156 Squadron, now that it was in Pathfinders, was 'We light the way', and the squadron's badge depicting Mercury, holding aloft a torch, left in no doubt what the task and function of this Pathfinder squadron was.

The village's name, Warboys, in Huntingdonshire, had an oddly resonant and appropriate ring to it, for those who brought their Wellingtons from Alconbury to an airfield near that village on August 5th and 6th really were boys at war, some of them fresh-faced, as boys ought to be, straight out of the Operational Training Units, while others of them looked old beyond their years, with dark rims under their eyes, veterans of the ceaseless process of peering into the dark skies over Germany. At Alconbury there had been no 'ops' on that month so far. On August 1st, six Wellingtons were standing by for 'ops' which were later cancelled. Met. had forecast fog on return. The same was true of the next day. Six aircraft stood by for 'ops', and then the cancellation came through. Meanwhile it was down to the training flights to continue preparations for 'ops', for, move or no move, Command expected a squadron to move and be ready for 'ops', and think nothing of it. And besides, despite the energetic pushing for a Pathfinder force to be created, it was not universally popular in Air Ministry circles, or even with the C. in C. himself.

W/C R. N. Cook, the Squadron Commander at Alconbury, was 'reposted' to command the squadron in its new role on August 2nd, and the very day when the move to Warboys was completed, August 6th, three Wellingtons operated to Duisburg and returned successfully. The first officially-led Pathfinder operation took place on August 18th to Flensburg. And yet, from the day when the move from Alconbury had been completed to this Flensburg attack 156 never really stopped operating. It was Osnabruck on August 9th, Mainz on the 11th when three 'experienced and first class crews' (captained by S/L Beavis, P/O Taylor and Sgt. Harker) failed to return, and Mainz again the next night when all ten aircraft returned. On the 15th out of eleven Wellingtons detailed for 'ops' on Dusseldorf, three were unready and could not be made operational, three returned early and one, captained by Sgt. Newlove, was shot down. The Warboys aircraft which did attack Dusseldorf that night navigated to the target on Gee, and attacked on E.T.A.

On August 17th all the squadrons designated as Pathfinders were on their aerodromes. The crews, flying Wellington IIIs at Warboys, Lancasters at Wyton, Stirlings at Oakington and Halifaxes from Graveley, were assured that there would be an 'op' that night, the maiden 'op' of the four Pathfinder squadrons. Instead, after the cancellation of operations, the *Operations Record Book* of 156 notes that 'a very successful party' was held in the Officers' Mess. It was time to celebrate and let off steam. The punishing schedule of the past few days, moving, continuous training, operating five times since the move, and losing four crews in that time had taken its toll. The Pathfinder maiden 'op' came the next night, August 18th. It was not an auspicious start. Of the thirty-one Pathfinder aircraft which set out from the four squadrons, the crews of sixteen claimed to have found the target. Eight Wellingtons, with their five man crews, set out from Warboys shortly after 8.00p.m. Two of the Warboys aircraft carried flares only, and belonged to the 'flare force'. Other Pathfinder aircraft carried incendiaries. The idea, in these early days, the 'stone age' of pathfinding, was not to mark the targets, but simply for the flare force to illuminate the target with the strings of flares they carried, backed up with incendiaries dropped by others on the aiming point, which, so the theory ran, could be discerned visually in the glare of the flares. No time for training, no resources yet developed to perfect flare marking. The Pathfinders went to war with rudimentary and dangerously volatile flares, far more dangerous to the aircraft that carried them than to the enemy. Of the two Wellington crews, carrying flares on the Flensburg operation, the crew of F/S T. E. Case had to abort the task soon after take-off. One flare had ignited in the aircraft, and, though the pilot instructed the bomb-aimer to jettison the flares immediately, some nevertheless ignited. For all this, the fiercely burning flares fell to earth and burnt themselves out close to a farm five miles from the aerodrome. No damage was done. The other flare-carrying Wellington, captained by F/L Greenup, had the unique distinction of being the first Pathfinder aircraft to cross the enemy coast, and reach the target. That was, however, as far as it went. The following report tells its own story of searching in the blackness and of not wanting to mislead the bombers on this first Pathfinder raid of the war:

'Flares only carried. Target not definitely identified. Searched for 15 minutes and unable to pinpoint due to haze and bad visibility. Did not drop flares in case main force should be misled thereby. 17 bundles of flares brought back'.

F/L Anderson formed a part of the five-man crew in F/L Greenup's Wellington that night. He had managed to obtain a ride in one of the Pathfinder Wellingtons on that first raid. At the time he was not on the Sqadron's strength, but on G/C Bennett's staff as a navigation officer, later the senior navigation officer. He had volunteered for aircrew after a desk job in the R.A.F., having been a schoolmaster before the war, and despite his being able to give most aircrew ten years, an inherent tendency to airsickness, and a suspect right eye, he became an efficient, and courageous 'press on' navigator, impressive enough to be poached by Don. Bennett, when Pathfinders were being established. In 1954, when he left the R.A.F., it was as W/C E. W. Anderson, O.B.E., D.F.C., A.F.C. He has written one of the first books to be written in the literature of Bomber Command on our subject, simply entitled *Pathfinders*, and published by Jarrolds one year after the war's ending. Written in the authentic Pathfinder idiom, so soon after the event it chronicles, it has a freshness, a sadness, and a rarity of expression which make it a classic. I devoutly hope it will soon be reprinted. In the darkness of that Flensburg night, with ground haze, difficult, unforecasted winds, and an absence of the sophisticated equipment that was later considered essential, it is not surprising that the accuracy and precision that made Pathfinders famous could not be effected. Also this night the first Pathfinder casualty occurred. One Halifax failed to return to Graveley. Happily Sgt. J. W. Smith and his crew became P.O.Ws.

Two days after Flensburg G/C Bennett visited Warboys and gave lectures to a group of aircrew gathered from various squadrons on Pathfinder aims and techniques. Six crews volunteered for Pathfinders as a result of these lectures, and the next day three new crews joined 156. On August 20th four Warboys aircraft flew in an operation to Frankfurt. Once more, as on the Flensburg raid, considerable difficulties were experienced by these Pathfinder crews in pinpointing a target under cloud and haze. All the Warboys aircraft returned, with one of them, captained by F/L McKenzie, landing at Abingdon. It was other Pathfinder squadrons who were hit this night. Five Pathfinder aircraft failed to return, including two Stirlings from Oakington. The next night, it was the turn of Warboys to be affected. Out of fourteen Wellingtons which took off for a raid on Kassel, four returned early, and three did not come back at all, the crews of F/S Savage, F/S Longhurst and of Sgt. James. These, the only Pathfinder casualties, fell victim to night fighters.

F/L Gilmour, it is recorded, made a 'very fine show in marking the target', a commendation which has a rather elegiac quality, seeing that he went missing two nights later on a raid to Nuremberg on his forty seventh operation, with F/L Spencer as second pilot (or 'second dicky' in R.A.F. parlance). The Nuremberg 'op' was a successful one for the Pathfinders. They used 'Red Blob Fires', a special type of incendiary that burnt an incandescent red, and for their efforts received a special commendation from the C. in C. Out of the twenty-three aircraft lost on this raid fourteen Wellingtons were lost (34 per cent of those sent out). Sixteen Pathfinder aircraft from all four squadrons had failed to return during this first month of the Pathfinders' history of operations. Four of the missing were from Warboys (counting, of course, August 18th as the start of Pathfinder operations), which had, however, lost a total of eight crews since the move from Alconbury on August 6th.

On September 1st the Pathfinders marked the wrong town, Saarlouis instead of Saarbrucken, thirteen miles away. The raid was not recorded as a failure, however, as some considerable industrial damage was done. On returning to base one of 156 Squadron's Wellingtons crashed at King's Ripton, killing three of the crew. The next night the Pathfinders, eighteen of them, rose to a high standard of accuracy in bombing Karlsruhe, although only three Warboys Wellingtons operated. After Karlsruhe, on the third anniversary of the outbreak of the war, the Padre, S/L Bullen, held a special service. A raid on Bremen, on September 4th saw the Pathfinder force divided into Illuminators, the leaders with their white flares, the Primary Visual Markers with coloured flares, and the Backers-Up, whose task was to drop incendiaries on the coloured flares. With each raid experiments were carried out, and improvements noted. The weather, however, was the perpetual problem. A raid on Frankfurt on September 8th, for example, in eight to ten-tenths cloud saw inaccurate Pathfinder marking, and most of the bombing fell fifteen miles away to the southwest of the target in the town of Russelsheim (thus inadvertently damaging Opel and Michelin factories). Meanwhile crews were arriving from other squadrons, something urgently needed at Warboys, since, on most raids, aircraft were intercepted by night fighters, so that, despite its tough geodetic construction, Wellington losses, and losses in aircrew, were correspondingly high.

Two crews were missing from a raid on Bremen on September 13th, captained by S/L Collier and Sgt. Brough while on an operation to Essen three nights later four of the seven Warboys Wellingtons fought desperate battles with German nightfighters. The aircraft of Sgt. Proudfoot crashed on return, and flares, previously thought to have been jettisoned, ignited and caused burns to some crew members. Over Saarbrucken on September 19th there occurred a celebrated exploit which was to bring 156 Squadron very much into the news.

It concerned a senior operational pilot, S/L 'Artie' Ashworth, a New Zealander, with a fashionable handlebar moustache, who gave the order to bale out as the flares he was carrying had ignited. Having ensured the safety of his crew, he then discovered, to his horror, that he could not find his parachute. After throwing the aircraft around the sky, he managed to put out the flames. S/L Ashworth then flew the Wellington back to England, trimming the aircraft from time to time (as the automatic pilot was damaged) while he dashed back to pick up navigation charts, to pull on controls handled by missing crew members, and to deal with all the demands that were customary when a full crew was present. Amazingly, he brought the Wellington down to land at West Malling. S/L Ashworth had been a member of the famous 75 Squadron, the New Zealand squadron, based at this time at Newmarket. Early in 1943 he left Warboys to go to H. Q. Pathfinder Force in Huntingdon as one of the staff officers. It was he who gave his name to the skymarkers used by Pathfinders, the skymarkers codenamed 'Wanganui' flares after his home town in New Zealand. G/C Bennett designated three kinds of Pathfinder marking attacks after the home towns of those present, *Newhaven* (a visual attack), based on the home town of the W.A.A.F. Corporal who acted as his Secretary, *Parramatta* (a blind ground marking attack) based on his own home town in Australia, and *Wanganui* a sky-marking attack by parachute flares, as already mentioned, based on S/L Ashworth's home town in New Zealand. After staff duties S/L Ashworth, D.S.O., D. F.C., A.F.C., resumed his distinguished operational career on 635 Squadron at Downham Market, when that came into service with the Pathfinder Force.

For the rest of the month there were no operations. An intensive training period filled the gap: night cross-country flights, bombing practice, air to air firing, instructional films. And there was always sport, which the R.A.F. believed in whole heartedly. 'A' flight groundcrew beat 'B' flight groundcrew 4 to 1, Navigators beat W/Ops 3 to 2, and the Squadron team beat S.H.Q. by 5 to 1. Pathfinders, it seemed, trained hard, operated hard, and played hard. The C. in C. did not want a '*corps d' élite*', when the question of the Pathfinders was mooted. He was, nevertheless, getting one. August and September had been costly to 156. High casualties did not, it is obvious, deter enthusiastic volunteers, for new crews were arriving on the squadron every few days. The training component, however, was relentless, as the Group Commander sought more and more to improve standards. Equipment too was all the time being improved, and new ways of finding and marking the target were being developed. H2S was being put to the test. H2S was a new radar aid to navigators which displayed impressions of built up areas, coastlines, and rivers on a cathode ray tube, all impressions being derived from signals received from the ground itself. Oboe aircraft, meanwhile, were training all the time, and would soon operate. 'Pink pansies', 4,000lb incendiary bombs igniting with a pink flash, had been used to mark the target over Dusseldorf on September 10/11th.

The weather, however, remained Pathfinder Force's implacable foe. Although the crews would go out again in the forthcoming October nights, the bad weather would make the last three months of 1942 a difficult, dangerous and occasionally fatal period for Bomber Command crew, including, especially, the Pathfinders, and among them the veteran Wellingtons and their crews on 156.

A supreme example of atrocious weather conditions occurred on October 5th when the Squadron sent 5 out of the 12 aircraft detailed on a raid to Aachen. The crews took off in a raging thunderstorm. Soon after they took off, one of the Wellingtons was seen to be on fire, and crashed at Somersham, after all the crew had baled out. Some cottages were set on fire, although no one was killed. On their return another Warboys Wellington crashed at Gestingthorpe, killing the pilot, Sgt. Chiddick, while the rest of the crew baled out. F/L Greenup's aircraft was struck by lightning on crossing the French coast. Jettisoning his flares, he turned for home, not, however, without being subjected to the most accurate and intense flak. The crew baled out, and yet F/L Greenup, unable to bale out himself, repeated the solo exploit of 'Artie' Ashworth a few weeks before, bringing the aircraft back to England to a crash landing at Manston. The next day Sgt. Chiddick's crew was retrieved by an aircraft from Warboys which flew to Stradishall, while another Wellington flew to Manston to pick up F/L Greenup. Thankfully, the seven aircraft which operated to Osnabruck that night all returned safely, with only one early return.

During the following week, when the bad weather compelled the squadron to stand down, a diversion of a different nature occurred on October 9th, when A/M Harris, the C. in C. visited Warboys, accompanied by the A.O.C. 3 Group, A/V/M Cochrane, and G/C Bennett, the Commander of the Pathfinder Force.

The Kiel raid on October 13th caused considerable damage. The glow, so the crews said, could be seen for 100 miles. Of the four aircraft which took off that night from Warboys, one failed to return, the Wellington captained by Sgt. J. Taylor. Of those Wellingtons who did get back, one landed at Martlesham and one at Wyton. Two nights later in a raid on Cologne, S/L Hobbs and his crew failed to return on their Wellington's first operational flight. Sadly, on this night, although the blaze had been started by the Pathfinder crews effectively and in the right place, many main force crews, swallowed up in thick haze, could not identify, with any degree of accuracy, the Pathfinder marking, and so bombed the centre of the wrong fires. To the bomb aimer from 12,000 feet up the distinctiveness of the pink pansies and the other indicatory markers was often completely obliterated. It became the task of the planners and researchers to eliminate this problem. No operations, due to the continuing bad weather, took place for the rest of the month, and on the 26th a new C/O, W/C Tommy Rivett-Carnac D.F.C., an able and energetic South African, popularly known as 'Nuts and Bolts', was posted to the squadron. On the 28th he took up his command, and W/C Cook, who had served the squadron efficiently and courageously in the difficult transition period, from a main force squadron at

Alconbury to a new role as a Pathfinder Squadron at Warboys, was posted to Hemswell.

There was a turning between late October and the end of November to Italian targets, in support of the invasion of North Africa. Thus Genoa was the target twice (October 22nd and 23rd), and Turin once on October 24th, but not for 156 Squadron, which had a general stand down for this latter part of the month. On November 7th Warboys sent nine aircraft to Genoa, a raid which was recorded as an outstanding success, for which all credit was bestowed on the Pathfinders, who marked the target expertly, and courageously. One Warboys aircraft failed to return, captained by W/O D. G. Chell. Two nights later nine aircraft successfully operated against Genoa from Warboys. The following night (November 9th) eight aircraft took off from Warboys to Hamburg, a raid in which unusual winds and cloud and haze made the task difficult. There were also two successful 'ops' to Turin (on November 13th and November 20th). No aircraft had to return early, and none failed to return. On November 22nd, it was back to a German target, Stuttgart, from which one aircraft, piloted by F/L E.A. Fletcher, did not return. That night the Wellington of Sgt. R. J. Wallis was hit by flak over the target, wounding two crew members, and the aircraft was attacked by a night fighter on the way back home. By another minor miracle, and by great and skilful airmanship, the Pathfinder Wellington was brought home to England, and a belly landing at Bradwell Bay.

On the Turin raid of November 28th the Pathfinders marked the aiming point so effectively that the Royal Arsenal, which was one of the briefed targets, was enveloped by explosions. All eight Warboys Wellingtons took off and returned.

A visit by G/C Bennett a few days before the Turin raid, on November 25th, was good for morale, though whether the navigation quiz he conducted for aircrew proved universally popular we cannot say. As December opened, it seemed as if the Squadron was passing through an almost unprecedented period of good fortune. Frankfurt (on December 2nd), Mannheim (on December 6th) and Turin (on December 8th and December 9th) were visited without sustaining any casualties among the squadron's Wellingtons. Sadly, this was to change. On a raid to Duisburg (on December 20th) W/O Watkins, and F/S Proudfoot, two experienced pilots, and their crews did not come back, while on the next night F/L Cybulski, one of the most senior operational pilots, was lost over Munich. There were no more operations that year. After 'ops' had been scrubbed on Christmas Eve, the festive season was celebrated with great enthusiasm, all the more so because it was realised that the Wellington, the faithful 'Wimpy', was on its way out for Pathfinder crews. On the last day of 1942 three Lancaster I aircraft arrived at Warboys, and conversion training began in earnest. A new era had arrived.

*A/C Bennett with
H.M. the King on the
visit to Warboys,
February 10, 1944*
(Taff Jones)

*Their Majesties
visit to Warboys
on February 10,
1944, with G/C
Collings (left) and
A/C Bennett (right).*
(Taff Jones)

14

H.M. the Queen shakes hands with F/L Manvell, D.F.M., the Squadron Engineering Officer, (who died on June 24, 1944) while W/C Eaton, the Squadron C.O., looks on. (Taff Jones)

A/C Bennett, H.M. the King, and G/C Collings leave one of the hangars after their inspection. (Taff Jones)

CHAPTER 3

R.A.F. WARBOYS:
THE SQUADRON ON THE EDGE
OF THE FENS

'And when the air force saw it,
It looked so sweet and fair,
They said, "That's what we're looking for,
We'll build our air force there." '

R.A.F. Song.

Warboys, whose name is a combination of Old Norman French and Anglo-Saxon, means 'Lookout Wood'. It stands on the edge of the fens, between St. Ives and Ramsey, and quite near to Huntingdon, among a region of eastern England noted for 'witchfinding' in the seventeenth century. Indeed it is the last place on record where a witch was hanged in this country. Its friendly people belie the image of witchcraft, however, and this small place with its parish church of St. Mary Magdalene, with its Methodist and Baptist churches, with the tall Victorian clocktower at one end of its main street, with its two schools and eight pubs, was to become during one period of the Second World War home to thousands of airmen, to many of them their last home. A village of approximately one thousand people where the chief treat for children was a Sunday School outing, and a picnic in the bluebell woods the other side of the village, was to become home to a host of young men and women, some of them of various nationalities. Warboys was about to undergo not only an 'invasion' but a kind of revolution. Class barriers in the village fell, as if they had never been. Homes were opened, and villagers walked down to the wire barrier over the road by the cemetery to watch those Lancasters, aircraft of tremendous dignity, take off in the late summer or in the fading light of day in another part of the year.

When war broke out, however, the people of Warboys were rather close, too close for some, to the pre-war R.A.F. station of Wyton, down the road to Huntingdon, and not far away from another pre-war station, Upwood, in the Ramsey direction. The aircraft that filled the skies in those days were

Blenheims, from Upwood, which housed an O.T.U., and, after those operational Blenheim squadrons came back to Wyton almost decimated from the Battle of France, Wellingtons from Wyton, and in 1941, Stirlings. Another airfield, as a second satellite for Wyton (she had Alconbury already), was badly needed, and surveyors from the Air Ministry decided that the soil of Warboys, adequately drained, could support a squadron of bombers, and, indeed the entire airfield establishment which housed and maintained that squadron. By mid-1941 R.A.F. Warboys was ready for use, and indeed housed Stirlings of 15 Squadron from Wyton instead of the expected Blenheims.

That was when Warboys was first operational. For two months, from October until half way through December, Warboys was a Stirlings aerodrome. Then the Blenheims of the O.T.U. occupied Warboys until 156 Squadron came from Alconbury in August of 1942, equipped with their Wellingtons.

During the Stirling period the villagers had it brought home to them what war was about. One time in November 1941 an aircraft failed to take off and crashed not far from the airfield. As bombs were still on board, it crashed with an explosion which rattled the windows for miles around. All children had to be evacuated in coaches, as there were some unexploded bombs which needed to be taken to a place of safety and detonated. The excitement, danger and dislocation were working into the soul, and auguring the shape of things to come. When 156 Squadron moved to the village, the transformation of Warboys was to become complete.

The village wondered what had hit it. Of course, in a sense, the revolution had started with the outbreak of the war, and the coming of the evacuees from blitzed London. The villagers were, on the whole, more apprehensive about the evacuees than they were about the R.A.F. Indeed, the people of the village of Warboys were to become proud of their Pathfinder squadron when it became domiciled on the nearby airfield. In the early months there was a little apprehension, not surprisingly when you reflect that this rural community was to have a sudden influx of R.A.F. personnel, which would eventually become a squadron establishment of 1,700 individuals. Shops thrived, except that tobacconists were always running out of cigarettes. Crews and groups of airmen adopted individual public houses. The landlord and his wife and the regulars in The Wheatsheaf, The Red Cow, The Ship, The Pelican or in The Stag and Hounds at Old Hurst, or in all the others, would grow fond of their new regulars and would feel genuine grief when one of 'their' crews went missing. At another extreme, boys from Saskatchewan, Durban, or North Wales would find a welcome in the Baptist or Methodist chapels or in St. Mary Magdalene out there on the very edge of the airfield. The W.V.S. dispensed cups of tea and cakes, serving them from a shop sited on the main street. Everyone wanted to help, to 'do their bit' for these boys. Of course the girls of the village were thrilled. There were dances on the aerodrome, and in the village hall, and families in the village opened their homes to the young airmen. Not a few good marriages were made among local girls, although, sadly, during the Pathfinder years, as losses mounted, especially during the Battle of the Ruhr (in early 1943) and the Battle of Berlin (in late 1943 and early 1944), some brides of a few months or weeks became widows, and Warboys had her share of these.

These circumstances, grimly evident in the broadcast figures of those who failed to return, in the unofficial 'gen' circulating in the pubs ('big chop night last night at the "drome" - three didn't come back'), which produced a crop of anxious telephone calls to the Sergeants' or Officers' Messes, caused the Warboys villagers to seek to cossett and protect 'our boys'. Nothing was too good for them. Meagre rations were shared, and cultures were mingling. Boys from the Welsh valleys or Nottinghamshire mining villages were learning the ways of the fens. And some of these young men came from further afield. The Pathfinders needed trained and experienced aircrew; so Warboys learned to entertain Canadians and Australians, New Zealanders and South Africans, and the occasional Czech, Pole or Belgian. This was the essential greatness of Bomber Command, and certainly of the Pathfinders, that aircrew from opposite ends of the globe could be welded into their little families of seven or eight who lived together, played together, and (it must be admitted) quite often died together.

It is amazing that so many aircrew were married, giving the evident and widely-known loss-rate they, and more especially the Pathfinders, sustained. To misapply Dr. Johnson's famous dictum (used by him of a second marriage) the frequent marriages of aircrew were indeed the 'triumph of hope over experience'. But hope, as we know, springs eternal and most, if not all aircrew, started out on their great adventure with the thought that, 'even though several around me go for a Burton, it will never happen to me'. And who would deny or grudge them a few weeks or months even of wartime married life? Wartime 'ops', with the familiarity of sudden death, added also their own urgency and immediacy to living. 'You'd be so nice to come home to', was the wartime song. So there was marriage, and there was giving in marriage, and though parents, with a quite proper protective instinct, would murmur that there's no future in it, their daughters, nevertheless, took their Pathfinder bridegrooms to be wed at St. Mary Magdalene's church at the very edge of the airfield, or at the Baptist or the Methodist churches further down the main street of the village; and, if anxieties multiplied, then so did those snatched hours of happiness, or for those who had wives in distant places those glorious leaves every six weeks.

Leaves were sacred. Even in the thick of 'ops' at times of big offensives, it was considered essential to let the men go on leave. Clean sheets, some luxuries, comradeship, a hospitable and admiring host population, and even perhaps a wife at home, were all of them factors which enabled the member of a Pathfinder squadron to go on, and on. There was a strange alchemy, a strange compulsion about bomber 'ops'. There was a feeling about not letting the side down, when you were tired, and afraid, and just hanging on, and at the other extreme there was the feeling that you just could not do without this life, that made you volunteer for Pathfinders, and an extended tour of 55 'ops', or made you chafe at being an instructor, and made you long to return to an operational crew, a close band of brothers, swapping gen in the mess about flying, the flak, the flares, the fighters, the route finding, the Met., the odds about hot targets and average targets, the 'gen' that Groupie or the WingCo had given at the briefing. Wives, girlfriends, family were a necessary part of you, but the crew, and then the squadron, in that order, were top priority. If the crew were split up, or members were shuffled (and this, perforce, often happened), then that was not liked. Crews went out together, officers and N.C.Os alike, and sergeants were on first name terms with squadron leaders. In the air a tightly-knit discipline supervened. Sloppy discipline could annihilate a crew. Every member knew their own jobs thoroughly; in theory they knew more than one job, and many were the times that one crew member took over the job of another, because that crew member was severely wounded, or killed, or unable to continue.

On their posting to Warboys, crew and individuals usually ended their journey from a variety of places at the graceful and old fashioned buildings of Huntingdon station, which was showing every sign of not being able to cope with the ebb and flow of wartime traffic and transport. At the station you telephoned Warboys and waited for a transport to pick you up, if there was not one there already. Meanwhile there were trucks there ferrying others to Graveley and Wyton. Huntingdon was alive with airmen. After being based at Wyton for a short spell, G/C Bennett, had his wartime H.Q. for the Pathfinder Force in Huntingdon at an eighteenth century residence on Castle Hill, Castle Hill House, and The George, an old coaching inn in the centre of the town, did a thriving trade in accommodating aircrew wives and girlfriends between leaves and when stand downs were on. St. Ives and, more distantly, Cambridge, were also the places to go to to celebrate survival, promotion, or the award of a 'gong', or simply to let off steam, and yet Huntingdon was not only the H.Q. for all the Pathfinder squadrons, but the entrance, the gateway to the squadrons.

You may well have had to wait a while for your transport at the railway station. When it came you may have known the W.A.A.F. or airman driver from the M.T. section. He or she may have driven you out to the dispersals for the last few 'ops'. You would then ask what had happened in the intervening six days since you had been at Warboys, and you would, all too often, learn that Smithie or Tiny or that voluble, dark French Canadian had gone missing. Worst of all, although in most cases crews went on leave together, you may (because of the exigencies and demands of crew shuffles) learn that you are crewless. That was a shattering experience. That was a family bereavement of a total and desolating kind.

Imagine, however, that you are completely new, and just starting out on the squadron as an aircrew member. The transport takes you and your kit up the present day A141 out of Huntingdon. A few miles out of the town you slow down, and the Bedford van clashes its brakes, for, ahead of you a number of trucks are turning off to enter R.A.F. Wyton off to the right. Wyton looks the superb, well-maintained, solid pre-war station it is. A surprise is in store for you, for Warboys is not like this at all. Alongside Wyton it seems and looks like a Cinderella. Rivalry between the crews of 156 and 83 Squadrons were fed by these features of comparison; as a Pathfinder station Wyton had always had Lancasters, whereas Warboys just had Wimpys, and converted to Lancasters in January 1943. Wyton sent out the first Bomber Command sortie, a Blenheim on photo reconnaissance, a few hours after the outbreak of war, whereas Warboys hosted for a two month period in 1941, like cuckoos in the nest, the Stirlings of 15 Squadron. Above all, whereas Wyton was planned, brick-built, and well-appointed, Warboys was dispersed, nissen hutted, and marooned in the mud.

The first sign of airfield habitation, after driving along the road past Wyton, was the sewage works on the left, very necessary on a site accommodating approximately 2,000. Cottages and houses of Old Hurst village are seen on the right, with nissen huts at the edge of the houses and in adjacent fields, as if the airfield was colonising the village, or living in some kind of uneasy symbiosis with it. These nissen huts were long, some of them, and not unpleasant looking. They almost seemed to merge into the trees. These were the billets and living accommodation for several categories of personnel, whether airmen, or N.C.Os or officers.

The truck moves on, and further along the same road nearer to Warboys, and, again, on the right, a jumble of buildings is encountered. One of them is a dining room, and there is the Officers' Mess and Sergeants' Mess. Further back from the road you can just make out the Station Commander's quarters, and a building which serves as a chapel and gym combined. Further on, along the right of the road, a huddled group of nissen huts form the station sick quarters. Last of all, at the far end of the road stands the Waafery, the site for the airwomen, and the thriving N.A.A.F.I..

Now you can see the airfield, looming ahead, on the left, Drawing up to the main gate, you see the sign R.A.F. Station Warboys, and just inside the barrier the shed, with the instruction that all visitors must report at this point. A clerk in this, the orderly room, asks for your papers, takes your details, and your billet is allocated. The driver, with an orderly accompanying, drives you back to one of the huts on the living quarters, which, of course, you passed when you came up by road. If you are an N.C.O., you are driven to a long nissen hut, one of several near to Old Hurst village, with a number of beds, 12 each side, or more, and beside every bed a steel locker. You may realise, as you put away your kit, and make conversation with another flight-sergeant, or warrant-officer, who is lounging on one of the beds, that up to that morning the bed you are about to sleep in was occupied by someone who did not return from last night's raid on Cologne. The 'Committee of Adjustment', as they were known, an officer (the

Adjutant, or the Padre sometimes, or sometimes another officer) together with one or two airmen, would have been in the hut, and even as those who were still sleeping off last night's raid were abed, would have folded up belongings and kit, and, after tactfully removing anything that was likely to offend, would have posted them to next of kin or would send them on to one of the central depositories in Slough or Uxbridge which housed the effects of missing aircrew. It was immediate. It was precise, as happens in the case of procedures that go on several times a week, week in and week out. It was, almost, clinical. It was just as though the aircrew member had never been. Everybody knew the bed would not be empty for long, a few hours in many instances. And, here you were, occupying a bed in the N.C.Os' hut, just after who knows how many passing guests (or ghosts) had occupied it over the past few months.

If you were an officer, then the truck that had dropped the N.C.Os it had picked up at Huntingdon station moved on a little further along the narrow concrete roads of the same domestic site. The hut you are allocated as an officer is smaller than the long nissen hut of the N.C.Os. There are six bedrooms, divided by partitions, with a bathroom at one end, and a room for your batman. The batman is discreet, and protective. He has to go on, too, like aircrew do, and groundcrew. He is another member of that enormous body of non-flying personnel who become attached to the aircrew, who come and go in such rapid succession. Other bedrooms in this officers' hut may be empty, awaiting newcomers. Sometimes an officer would wake up a morning after a raid to be told, gently, by the batman, that all the other bedrooms in the hut were unoccupied. S/L 'Sam' Hall found himself in this situation when one of the flight commanders, W/C John White and his crew, all officers, were shot down on the first of the Autumn Berlin raids of November, 1943. Some endured until the replacements came, others, like F/L Basil Leigh, set operator in S/L Hopton's crew, packed his belongings and moved elsewhere. This was during one of the bad spells of January 1944 when 156 Squadron lost 15 aircraft in a single week.

As soon as you had seen your belongings safely stowed away, you sought to meet up with your crew, if you had a crew, or with other aircrew, if you were a solitary posting. In either event, you gravitated towards your mess. The messes were a place to meet in, relax in, have a drink in, and eat in, although there were other dining rooms, and eating places. Like the sleeping accommodation, the Sergeants' Mess was larger than the Officers' Mess. It was very long, and was divided into two. One part, an ante-room, had chairs, some of them quite comfortable, small tables with ash trays, and two fireplaces. There would be many N.C.Os in the Mess at early evening, and you could buy a drink in the bar in the ante room. The rest of the Mess was taken up with dining room and kitchen. The Officers' Mess had a similar pattern, except that it was smaller, and had a large billiard table at one end of the ante room. There was also a small side room where quieter conversations could be held. As in the case of the

Sergeants' Mess, the Officers' Mess possessed also its own kitchen and dining room. Those who were flying that night drank lemonade or soft drinks. On squadron stand downs, and on special party occasions, the messes would be full. Sometimes the mess parties would be wild, and games would be played which sent C.Os and senior flight commanders hurtling through the air. Much beer was drunk (although most of it was of far smaller strength than the ales of nowadays), and the usual songs were sung, *My brother Sylveste* and *The Muffin Man*. Such parties often helped the new arrivals to settle in, and meet fellow officers or N.C.Os. As the new arrivals came to replace others who had gone to an uncertain destination in the previous few days, they served as an important safety valve.

In fact not infrequently such parties on general squadron stand downs were often 'wakes', when so many friends had been lost, including often those 'old timers', all of twenty-four or twenty-five, whom you had begun to think were invulnerable. A description, graphic and moving, of one such party, held in the Officers' Mess in Warboys late in January, 1944, can be read in Chaz Bowyer's *Path Finders at War* (Ian Allan 1977, pp. 122 *ff*). The Squadron C.O., W/C Eaton, newly arrived, and destined not to have a long future, allows considerable liberties to be taken. There is something about aircrew at play which has an almost Homeric quality about it.

The next morning new arrivals, whether crewed or not, would meet in the crew room along with all the other flying personnel on the squadron. An informal gaggle of aircrew at 0900 hours would meet their C.O., and be told what flights and training details were on for that day. These daily meetings, called 'Morning Prayers' by aircrew, were, in spite of this nickname, most informal. New arrivals who had served on other squadrons would be amazed at the informality. Flight commanders would keep a close eye on new crews, and, in the case of single, unattached aircrew members, would assign them a crew, if they had not already been approached in the mess the night before by someone lacking a W/Op or a gunner, or otherwise weave them into their flight.

This, or something very like this, was the introduction to life at R.A.F. Warboys for an aircrew member recently arrived. At almost any time in the history of the squadron, from the Wellington period until the months after the invasion in 1944, by which time 156 Squadron had moved to Upwood, newly arrived aircrew would gain no comfort from asking the question uppermost in the minds of many, 'What is the rate of missing aircraft? So this was the one question they refrained from asking. The answer they knew already. Excitement, camaraderie, the terrific pride of being on Pathfinders, the highly technical nature of the job, which demanded considerable training and prolonged operational expertise - all these things combined to remove or to thrust to the dusty lumber room of buried anxieties a not unnatural apprehension. And anyway, as the extroverts among them cheerfully concluded, 'It will never happen to me'. The more thoughtful among them amended this: 'It may happen to me – but not yet, not for ages'. Meanwhile there's today, and tomorrow, and the day after that, and . . . who knows?

W/C Grant and his crew. Taken at Warboys in October, 1943. (Taff Jones)

F/L Terry Kearns and his crew. Taken at Warboys. (Taff Jones)

CHAPTER 4

THE RUHR AND HAMBURG

'There was flak, flak,
As much as you could pack,
In the Ruhr, in the Ruhr,
There was flak, flak,
As much as you could pack,
In the valley of the Ruhr.

My eyes are dim, I cannot see,
The searchlights they are blinding me,
The searchlights they are blinding me.'

(Aircrew popular song)

The first days of 1943 saw the conversion process from the Wellington Mark III to the Lancaster Mark I carried on in real earnest. This conversion process was drawn out by the inclement weather, so that the last Wellington operations flown by 156 were on January 15th, to Lorient, and on January 23rd to the same target. These attacks on Lorient were considered by the C. in C. to be a diversion from the real business of bombing Germany. They had been requested by the Admiralty to counter the U-boat menace and agreed by the War Cabinet so that Lorient and other operational U-boat bases on the French coast received a pounding. The aircraft of 156 had been detailed to attack Berlin on the night of the 17th; but the 'op' was scrubbed at 4.00p.m., not long before take-off. It was this Berlin raid that Richard Dimbleby flew on as a passenger in W/C Guy Gibson's Lancaster from 106 squadron. Over at Elsham Wold my father, flying as flight-engineer to Roley Newitt, reports in his log book:
'Very heavy and intense and accurately predicted "flak" over target; also much fighter activity'.
The previous night, January 16/17th, had also been a Berlin raid, and although 156 was not involved, other Pathfinder aircraft from other squadrons were, and 'modern', up-to-date T.Is were used for the first time. It was also the first time that Pathfinder aircraft had led a raid on Berlin, a feature of Pathfinder operating which would dominate the later part of 1943, and early 1944.

G/C Bennett was trying out the new strategy of blind marking. Other aircraft had led small, exploratory raids on Dusseldorf on New Year's Eve, and a string of Oboe trials was conducted against Essen, led by three or four Oboe Pathfinder Mosquitoes, on January 3rd, 4th, 7th, 9th, 11th, 12th and 13th.

The first operation for 156 in the squadron's new Lancasters was, again, to Lorient on January 26th, when four aircraft operated and all returned safely. The next night was to Dusseldorf, when of the four Warboys Lancasters detailed for 'ops', one returned early, and the other three returned safely. On this night five Oboe Mosquitoes of 109 Squadron used 'ground markers', those target indicators so recently introduced, which were set and fused to burst just above the ground, and then to cascade to earth. Three nights later, on January 30th, five Warboys aircraft took off for Hamburg. Pathfinder Stirlings from Oakington and Halifaxes from Graveley used H2S for the first time on operations, and the Warboys Lancasters were the 'backers-up', dropping their red flares with green stars. One aircraft returned early; but, again, 156 suffered no casualties.

January was a month of tentative moves for both squadron and Pathfinder Force in general. The working up to Lancasters, the use of new marking devices, the introduction of Oboe - all these took place during January, laying the pattern of 156 Squadron's agenda for the future. On January 25th the news came through that Pathfinder Force was to be promoted to the status of a Group, 8 Group, G/C Bennett was to remain the Group Commander, only with a promotion to Air Commodore, and the H.Q. of the Pathfinder Force in Huntingdon, now that it was a Group Headquarters, would need an increase in staff establishment. Several tour-expired officers from 156 served on the staff at Group H.Q. in Huntingdon. These were inevitably short postings, as the Group Commander neded to surround himself with those staff officers whose operational expertise was fresh and up to date.

The last day of January, the first casualty free month for some time for 156 (and one in which only two crews were lost from the whole of the Pathfinder Force) was marked by squalls of rain, and a strong gale blowing which made 'ops', and indeed any kind of flying impossible. There were many more operations carried out in February, and the weather was much better. Remarkably, there was to be only one aircraft from 156 Squadron which failed to return during this month. Two attacks were carried out on Lorient, two on Cologne, two on Wilhelmshaven, while the Italian targets were not neglected (Turin was raided on the 4th, and Milan on the 14th). Hamburg, Bremen, and Nuremberg were also visited, while on the last day of the month, St. Nazaire, another French U-boat base, was hammered. This list of targets is Bomber Command's war in microcosm, although we have to wait until the first day of the next month for a raid on Berlin, and, of course, the Ruhr battle was to start very shortly. The squadron was all the time sending out small numbers of aircraft, four, five or six at the beginning of February, nine or ten at the end of the month. The one crew casualty of February was the Lancaster of F/S T. E. Case, which did not come back from a raid on Wilhelmshaven on February 19th. F/S Case had been with the squadron from the very beginning, and had been through a number of 'shaky-do's' since the early Wellington days in August and September 1942. It was, so the other crews agreed, 'bad luck' to go like this, in a light period, on what, by Ruhr or Berlin standards, was a 'soft' target, or, as we would say, using our gift of hindsight, in the lull before the storm.

The storm about to break on Bomber Command in general, and on Pathfinder Force, was to cause crew after crew to disappear. It was like the Berlin offensive later in the year, this Battle of the Ruhr, except that it caused a greater and more effective degree of damage to the Ruhr towns than the corresponding series of raids did to Berlin. Now the crews started to fall from the night sky over the Ruhr. The offensive started on March 5th, and from that date until well into July the battle raged.

In his memoirs, *Bomber Offensive*, Sir Arthur Harris mentions that, now that Bomber Command was equipped, her 'main offensive' began. Moreover this offensive began at a precise time, the night of March 5th, 1943, when Oboe Mosquitoes marked the centre of Essen. It was a superb and perfect example of blind marking, performed and carried out by 109 Pathfinder Squadron, the Mosquito squadron which shared Wyton with No. 83 Lancaster squadron. Warboys sent eleven aircraft that night as 'backers-up'. They reported variously on their return, and yet all testified to the heavy flak co-operating with cones of searchlights. Extensive damage was done, especially to the Krupp factories. The thirty-five Pathfinder aircraft (including those from Warboys) had marked through thick industrial haze, in what the jargon called a *Musical Parramatta* attack, *Parramatta* after the Group Commander's home town in Australia being code for blind marking, with the adjective *musical* referring, in the code, to the fact that the attack was led by Oboe controlled aircraft. There was no gap between the marking aircraft, the marking was backed up, and the main force of 407 aircraft followed up in three waves in a 40 - minute attack.

That night was a turning point of the war. Admittedly Essen and other Ruhr targets were within the range of Oboe, whereas more distant targets (and several were attacked during this period) were not. It was now established, forthwith, however, that one of the most important of Germany's industrial cities could be hit accurately and damaged, cloud and industrial haze notwithstanding. This was the first raid really to hurt Essen, and it, and the succeeding raids on the Ruhr in the period from March to July, in what has become known as the Battle of the Ruhr, sent shock waves radiating through Germany.

The crews could not share in the euphoria of the planners. Oboe Mosquito crews were justifiably proud of what they had achieved. The Essen attack of March 5th was the culmination of their training, it was what all the practice flights out from Wyton, and the tentative feints had been leading up to. For the crews of the heavies the visits night after night to Ruhr towns, and other 'hot' targets, were a test of nerve and courage, and good crews were disappearing all too quickly. Fourteen aircraft failed to return from this first Essen attack. Among them was the Lancaster of S/L Hookway, D.F.C., of 156, a senior operational pilot and flight commander, who had assumed temporary command of the squadron for a few days some weeks previously, when W/C Rivett-Carnac had had to spend a brief spell in the R.A.F. Hospital in Ely.

Three nights later Nuremberg was attacked, and F/S White, D.F.M., failed to return from the nine aircraft operating from Warboys. The next night, March 9th, F/L Goodly did not get back from Munich among the seven Lancasters dispatched. Attacks, as had been indicated, were made well outside the Ruhr area, as well as those repeated attacks inside what aircrew called 'Happy Valley'. So, as we have seen, Nuremberg and Munich were attacked during this period, German cities far to the south. So too was Stuttgart on March 11th. Nor were targets in the north neglected. Kiel, Stettin and Berlin were raided. Just before the Ruhr offensive began with that dramatic Essen attack, Berlin had been attacked on March 1st. That had been a 'first' for 156 Squadron, and happily for them there were no casualties out of the nine aircraft dispatched. Well into the Ruhr offensive another attack was made on the 'Big City' on March 27th and eleven Warboys aircraft participated. From this raid by 396 aircraft nine failed to return, among them Sgt. Wallis and his crew from Warboys. They were old-timers on the squadron, and had had a dramatic return from a raid on Stuttgart in November of the previous year, as outlined in chapter two. On March 12th there was another successful Essen attack, led by the Oboe Mosquitoes, and with the Krupps factory again taking yet more damage. The third Essen attack, on April 3rd, was better still in terms of results obtained. Out of the twenty-one aircraft lost, a newly arrived Australian Sgt. Byass, and his crew did not get back to Warboys. The next night, April 9th, a raid to Kiel saw two Warboys aircraft shot down, those of S/L Grimston, D.F.C., and P/O Davies and their crews. S/L the Honourable Brian Grimston, D.F.C., known to 156 crews as 'the Honourable Grimmy', was so tall that he fitted with difficulty in the Wellington he flew in 1942, and was more comfortable in a Lancaster. A direct hit by flak over Kiel blew up his aircraft and crew. One by one the crews who had converted at the end of the previous year from Wellingtons to Lancasters were disappearing.

Of course the Squadron needed replacements all the time. Just before the Ruhr offensive started S/L John White joined 156. He was to remain with the Squadron for the greater part of the year, and to become one of the most successful and inspiring of operational captains. Sadly his luck ran out on the first raid of the Battle of Berlin at the other end of the year, November 18th, and when he died he was a Wing Commander, and a flight commander, with a D.F.C. On April 6th two pilots with their crews joined 156 among these replacements. Three crews had gone in the previous few nights, and the Squadron, in the face of repeated 'ops' and casualties, needed to maintain its strength and momentum. The two pilots were Sgt. Waugh, fresh from 1656

C.U., with his crew, and F/L Syd Cook, and his crew, from 103 Squadron, Elsham Wolds. Like John White, Syd Cook was to become one of those legendary pilots who, with his crew, were thought to be 'lucky', and who were, in the estimation of the aircrew, bound to survive. Don. Charlwood introduces him as a fellow Australian in his book *No Moon Tonight*, and as the captain with whom Harry Wright, another Australian, his friend, and Cook's navigator, flew. Just before John White died over Berlin, Syd. Cook, S/L A. S. Cook, D.F.C., D.F.M, perished in a raid on Frankfurt, on October 4th. Harry Wright was sick that night, and so survived, to write a novel about his experiences at Warboys, *Pathfinders Light the Way*, published in Brisbane in 1983. The other crew posted to Warboys on April 6th, captained by Sgt. Waugh, lasted only twenty days, failing to return from Duisburg on April 26th.

On April 16th out of thirteen aircraft detailed for 'ops' ten took off to bomb the Skoda armaments factory in Pilsen, Czechoslovakia. This raid has been held up as an example of mistaken Pathfinder marking, since many crews mistook a building at nearby Dobrany for the Skoda works, which featured as the aiming point. The Pathfinders were supposed to release T.Is not as markers on the target, but as guides to light up the way to the aiming point beyond. Main force bombers bombed their T.Is, and so an asylum building at Dobrany was bombed, and the Skoda factory was not at all hit. There were many night fighters around, and thirty-six aircraft were shot down (a shattering eleven per cent of the force dispatched). Out of the ten aircraft which Warboys finally sent that night two failed to return, one captained by W/O Anderson and the other by Sgt. Gonce. One squadron in 6 Group, 408 Squadron from Leeming (G/C Bennett's old base) lost four out of its twelve Halifaxes.

Another city that was proving a hot target was Duisburg. It was raided four times during the Battle of the Rhur, on March 26th, April 8th, April 26th, and May 12th. The first of those four raids was a casualty- free one, as far as 156 Squadron was concerned. On the second raid (April 8th) F/S Younger and his crew failed to return out of eight Warboys aircraft dispatched, Sgt. Waugh and his crew (who were posted to the squadron the same day as Syd. Cook and his crew) did not return from the April 26th raid, while two crews did not come back from the raid of May 12th, the Lancasters captained by S/L Verdon-Roe, D.F.C., and by Sgt. Wendon. S/L Verdon-Roe had been a young pilot officer when he had reported for duty at Warboys the day after the great move from Alconbury, on August 7th, 1942. He was the last of the 'old timers', the men who had fought in Wellingtons, and he was a member of the family of A. V. Roe, the company which produced the Lancaster. On that raid, on which he and the crew captained by Sgt. Wendon perished, 572 aircraft had visited Duisburg, which was, at that time, the largest inland port in Europe. Extensive damage was done, including acres of devastation in the port area itself.

In the Ruhr, most German towns were getting the Essen treatment. Dortmund was attacked on May 4th by 596 aircraft. This was, to date, the largest raid outside the 1,000 bomber raids of the previous year, and cost the Command thirty-one bombers which did not return, among them yet another senior pilot from the Wellington era, S/L Alastair Lang, D.F.C., and his crew from Warboys, although three of the crew, including the pilot, survived being shot down. At first the Pathfinder marking was good, but there was a good deal of undershooting, and fires lit by the enemy to decoy aircraft had a partial success. When the returning bombers were approaching their home bases, many of them had to be diverted to other airfields due to the deteriorating weather. Two returning aircraft crashed at Warboys, blocking the runway, and injuring the pilots. A senior pilot, an Australian, who had come with the new replacements a short time before, S/L 'Digger' Duigan, D.F.C., baled out over Chatteris with his entire crew. The weather was atrocious, the visibility nil, and the Lancaster had registered no fuel for some time. The abandoned aircraft plunged to earth, crashed and burnt out in the fens, away from human habitation. S/L Duigan's aircraft was one of the seven which crashed in the bad weather on returning home. Dortmund was visited later that month, on May 23rd, in a raid which was the largest of the Battle of the Ruhr, with 826 aircraft operating, and with Warboys dispatching a record number (to date) of twenty-two aircraft, all of which returned safely. The next night but one, May 25th, twenty-one Lancasters from Warboys operated to Dusseldorf. The squadron was operating with an ever increasing tonnage of bombs and flares. Yet there was more. From this month of May, some of the Lancasters of Warboys were equipped with an H2S cupola instead of with the ventral turret previously provided, and intensive training in the new marking medium was taking place. Day after day the *Operations Record Book* itemizes eight, four, three, two 'Y' training flights until, by the end of the month, large numbers of crews had become thoroughly proficient in operating the H2S set, and marking by means of it. Before 156 Squadron received new H2S aircraft, all the marking and illuminating on H2S had been carried out by the Stirlings of 7 Squadron and the Halifaxes of 35 Squadron. H2S aircraft were required to fly straight and level, and, in this time of testing and trying, flak batteries sought out these aircraft and, all too often, blew them out of the skies above the Ruhr and other targets. Oakington and 7 Squadron, one week in June, lost three flight commanders, flying in H2S- equipped Stirlings. The Oboe Mosquitoes did the work of primary blind marking where the targets were within Oboe range. Beyond these targets, it was up to the H2S aircraft of 7 and 35 Squadrons to provide the blind marking. Now, at the end of May, and the beginning of June, 156 and 83 used H2S- equipped Lancasters. That was why, by mid-June, there was a respite for 7 Squadron, and it was taken out of the front line to convert to Lancasters.

On May 27th it was back to Essen. Twenty- three out of the 518 aircraft dispatched did not return, among them the Lancaster captained by F/S Wallace of 156. He and his crew had only come to the squadron in the middle of April from 1656 conversion unit. F/S Wallace, an Australian, perished at the controls of his aircraft. There were four survivors from his crew, who became P.O.Ws, among them Jim Twinn, the bomb aimer, who is now a retired Head-Master, and Methodist Minister, and functions as the squadron padre. The outstanding raid of the month of May, however, came two days after the Essen raid. On May 29th, Wuppertal was attacked by 719 aircraft. For the first time, 156 Squadron, among the seventeen aircraft which reached the target, provided H2S aircraft, and these 'Y' aircraft, as they were called in code (remember the expression 'Y' training flights'), kept the red T. Is dropped by the Oboe Mosquitoes thoroughly backed up. Indeed, there was one interval in the Oboe marking, when, because of equipment failure, no reds were visible. It was therefore left to the 'Y' aircraft of 83 and 156 Squadrons to keep the aiming point constantly marked. This they did, and brought the raid to an extremely successful conclusion. There were no losses that night from Warboys; sadly 35 Squadron, at Graveley, lost four Halifaxes. This was out of a total loss by the Command of thirty-three aircraft. It is worth noting that successful marking and supporting on any raid often went hand in hand with significant Pathfinder casualties.

W/C William Anderson, known to all R.A.F. contemporaries as 'Andy', reflects in his book, *Pathfinders*, published shortly after the war (and alluded to in chapter 2), that, just as the Flanders poppy became symbolically the flower of sorrow for the generation of the Great War, so for the aircrew of Bomber Command, and their relatives, the appropriate symbol of remembrance could be the may blossom that we see in the hedgerows in the spring of the year. At the height of the Ruhr battle, Andy would wait in vain night after night for this or that aircraft to return, and, when it was obvious that the aeroplane and crew would not get back, would walk back from the dispersals to his own quarters seeing the white may blossom in the hedges nearby.

It was not all German targets of the fiercest kind. The enemy must not be allowed to concentrate his forces all in one area or battle front. Just as the bombers, therefore, reached out for those towns and cities further afield to the north and deep in the south, so were Italian targets visited. The docks at La Spezia were raided twice in April (on the 13th and the 18th), while at the very end of the battle, on July 12th, twenty-one Lancasters set out from Warboys to Turin, F/S Hewerdine and his crew failing to return. After Turin there was a raid on Aachen the next day (July 13th). Warboys did not send out any aircraft on this raid, and after this there was a pause in the relentless nightly raids, before the bombers reached out for Hamburg, and a new 'battle'.

It is time to turn briefly from battles and flights to people. For, among those joining the squadron at this time were a number of young men who were to stamp their personalities on the squadron, and who, whether they lived or died, were to be remembered for a long time to come. On April 27th a New Zealander, F/L Mandeno, reported for flying duties from 19 O.T.U. By August he was a Squadron Leader with a D.F.C., and a reputation for bringing back impossibly damaged Lancasters and their crews from a variety of targets. It was possible to walk over to the dispersals and see ground crews working simultaneously on two 'pranged' Lancasters that 'Mandy' Mandeno had flown back to Warboys on two successive nights. 'Mandy will always get back' became a watchword on the squadron.

The night Mandy won his D.F.C., June 11th, was a classic. It was a raid on Munster carried out only by Pathfinder aircraft, seventy-two of them, to test out the new H2S sets. F/L Mandeno was one of the twenty-one that took off from Warboys. As soon as he had taken off he realised that his Air Speed Indicator was useless. Nevertheless, he pressed on, with his navigator calling out the ASI reading at regular intervals. This, however, was bound to prevent full evasive action, and, when he was attacked by an ME110, the Lancaster was seriously handicapped. The cannon of the enemy aircraft hit the Lancaster in the tail, and yet the ME110 had to break off the engagement, when the rear gunner damaged it with two two-second bursts. Even so the enemy aircraft came in again, and was again damaged, this time severely, by further bursts from the rear gunner. In the earlier tangle with the ME110 the mid-upper gunner had his helmet blown off by the enemy's cannon, and fell from his turret inside the aircraft, injuring himself.

After the ME110 broke off the engagement because of severe battle damage, there now began the struggle to control the crippled Lancaster. As the Munster searchlights were, by now, in sight, F/L Mandeno pressed his attack home, with the help of the flight engineer. The H2S set had been smashed by the cannon fire of the Messerchmitt. Fortunately the target could be seen visually in the light of flares and in the bright, cloudless night, and so was bombed. The aircraft's T.Is and flares were, however, jettisoned near Cleve and so the crippled Lancaster was lightened still further. F/L Mandeno found that he could retain control over his aircraft at 140 knots and brought home the Lanc. to a very successful landing at Warboys. Out of the seventy-two Pathfinder aircraft taking part in what was really a mass H2S trial five aircraft failed to return, among them a Lancaster from Warboys piloted by F/S Lay. On June 25th F/L Mandeno was granted an immediate award of the D.F.C. Mandy finished his rather hectic tour just before Christmas 1943, and survived the war to transfer to the R.N.Z.A.F. in July 1945. His Canadian WOp/AG, P/O Al Fast D.F.M., married a W.A.A.F. on the station, Cpl. Nell MacLachlan, in Warboys Methodist church, and both now reside in Langley, British Colombia.

Another New Zealander who joined the squadron at about this time was F/L H. R. Hall, known to all his R.A.F. contemporaries as 'Sam' Hall. Sam was a navigator, had done a tour in 1940 on Wellingtons, with 1X Squadron at Honington, and took a drop in rank, from Squadron Leader to Flight Lieutenant, in order to return from instructional duties to operations. Sam Hall came over to Warboys from a temporary posting on 405 Vancouver Squadron which had just joined the Pathfinders and had moved to the new station at Gransden Lodge south of Cambridge. He came to Warboys on June 9th with the new squadron

C.O., G/C 'Ray' Collings, A.F.C. G/C Collings, a pre-war test pilot, and English bobsleigh champion, was a career R.A.F. officer, who was to be both C.O. and Station Commander for some of the most critical months in the squadron's history. F/L Hall was soon to become S/L Hall and thus receive back his old rank, to fly as navigator with two captains and crews, who perished, when flying with other navigators, to fly a number of operations as the C.O.'s navigator, and to become the Squadron Navigation Officer. A posting on to the staff of Bomber Command H.Q., High Wycombe just before Christmas followed, and a lengthy period of distinguished service with the R.A.F. from which he retired as G/C Hall, O.B.E., D.F.C.

On May 11th Sgt. John Sloper and his crew were posted to Warboys from 100 Squadron at Grimsby. Sam Hall flew as John Sloper's navigator on one trip, and he endeared himself to many personnel on the station. His groundcrew were particularly devoted to him for a hundred and one acts of consideration and courtesy. John Sloper was made for the role of the 'parfit, gentle knight', and he finished a tough, hard tour just before Christmas as F/L Sloper, D.F.C. Tragically he perished at the controls of a Lancaster flying from Warboys on April 10th, 1944, as an instructor in the Pathfinder N.T.U. For reasons eluding the investigators, the tail fin fell off the Lancaster, and the entire crew perished, along with W/C J. D. Green who was flying in the aircraft. A plaque in Welsh slate in memory of F/L J. L. Sloper, D.F.C., has been placed in the church of St. Mary Magdalene, Warboys, the church close to the airfield perimeter fence.

On May 25th F/L 'Vin' Vincent and his crew were posted to Warboys from 1662 conversion unit at Blyton. Vin Vincent had a large number of flying hours in his log book, and yet had a green crew, with one exception, Sam Hall, who flew with him as his navigator for fifteen 'ops', after which Sam became Squadron Navigator Officer, and F/L Vincent was assigned another navigator. Having done his first tour on Wellingtons in 1940, S/L Hall (he attained his old rank again shortly after joining 'Vin' Vincent's crew) noticed just how different the night skies over Germany were in mid-1943. Crews were now used to the lingering smell of cordite as the flak reached up to annihilate them, and the rattle of spent shrapnel on a Lancaster's fuselage was a commonplace occurrence. F/L Vincent's aircraft returned on several occasions with only three engines.

One other significant feature of 156 Squadron life, which Sam Hall recalls at the time he joined Vin Vincent's crew, was the equipping of squadron crews with H2S. Navigators of the new H2-S equipped aircraft had to interpret difficult and uncertain visual impressions on the cathode ray tube housed in the aircraft. About the only things that could be distinguished with certainty on the early sets were coast-lines, the outlines of river estuaries and large rivers, and the dense mass of housing constituting a major city. Moreover, since the equipment lacked stabilised aerials, the pilot needed to hold the aircraft straight and level. Most bombers weaved constantly on their progress to a target, and on their return, a manoeuvre which made it hard for German night fighters to get a fix on them with their A.I. (Airborne Interception) sets. 'Vin' Vincent was determined to use H2S in the fullest possible sense, and to obtain the maximum advantage from it. Not flying straight and level gave you better prospects for finishing a tour. Flying straight and level must enable you to hit the aiming point with great accuracy with the help of this newly acquired special equipment. F/L Vincent, being a robust, 'press on' type, announced his intention, on the run up to the target over Berlin, of holding the Lancaster straight and steady until the bomb aimer could see the aiming point. This news was greeted with a stunned reaction on the part of the crew. Straight and level over Berlin was suicide. Even so, 'Vin' Vincent steered into the flak barrage, straight as a dye. Finally, the rear gunner broke the silence, and, in a voice that barely disguised its tremor, blurted out: 'Couldn't you weave, skipper? Just a little bit?'. (This was on the first Berlin raid for some time, August 23rd, when fifty-six aircraft were lost, 7.9 per cent of the force of 727 aircraft dispatched).

On the next Berlin raid (September 3rd) F/L Vincent decided to press on, even after one of the two generators in the Lancaster became unserviceable. After bombing the target, the remaining generator was damaged and rendered u/s by a flak burst, reducing the aircraft to functioning without any radio or navigational aid. And yet, as the rear gunner said to a friend at debriefing back at Warboys, 'It was pretty rough. Both our generators were u/s on the way back. But it was O.K. Our navigator brought us back by 1940 methods'. Sam Hall used the methods of the 'old days' back in 1940, when there were no navigational aids. With the only torch in the aircraft, S/L Hall concentrated on his flight plan and after making adjustments to it, based on the winds calculated on the journey to the target, gave the pilot a course which brought them back just ten minutes behind E.T.A., and ten miles out of the expected landfall. Warboys was found by using all available signs, aerial lighthouses, and ground beacons flashing the coded letters of airfields, and, once over home, identification was established and identity confirmed by means of an Aldis lamp.

In the middle of the year, while the Ruhr battle was still raging, one night later than the celebrated Munster raid from which 'Mandy' Mandeno had made so dramatic a return, Bochum, an important middle-ranking Ruhr town, was raided. This was a casualty-free night, as far as Warboys was concerned, but twenty-four were lost out of the entire bomber force of 503, which is 4.0 per cent. Bochum was accurately marked by the Oboe method, and 130 acres were devastated. Every raid on a Ruhr target was now counting, for all the losses. A few days later, three Warboys Lancasters were missing from a raid on Cologne, those of S/L J. C. Mackintosh, W/O Busby and Sgt. Miller. W/O Busby had flown on the Munster raid with Vin Vincent as 'second dicky' to give him experience, while S/L Mackintosh had joined the squadron as an experienced test pilot, and had been Sam Hall's first pilot when he came to Warboys. That night Sam Hall was on leave, and S/L Mackintosh had taken another navigator to Cologne. Krefeld and Mulheim were raided in the later June days. From

Krefeld F/S Marson did not come back, while F/S Winterbon failed to return from Mulheim. Sixty per cent of Mulheim was destroyed in this one raid, at a cost of thirty-five aircraft. Another raid, notable for the accuracy of the Pathfinder marking, took place on June 24th. Wuppertal was raided (the second time since May), and this time the Elberfeld section of Wuppertal was destroyed, just as in May the Barmen half of the town had been devastated. And yet, out of 630 aircraft, thirty-four were missing, two of them Warboys Lancasters, captained by W/O L. F. J. Brown, and P/O R. J. Hudson.

After three further attacks on Cologne (on June 28th and July 3rd and 8th), the first of which was Cologne's worst raid of the entire war, the Ruhr offensive ended in the second week of July, with the raids on Turin (July 12th) and Aachen (July 13th) already mentioned. For the next few days there were no operations but a thoroughgoing period of training, including 'Y' flights, air to air firing, bombing practice, beam training and cross country flights. The constant emphasis on every training opportunity for the crews of 156 was a practice flight, using the H2S set, fitted in every squadron Lancaster one month before. It is continuous 'Y' training day after day in the *Operations Record Book* on every day that could be spared from operations. And meanwhile, with the Pathfinder Lancasters fitted with H2S sets, and with the new device code-named 'Window' about to be introduced, the C. in C. and his staff were looking towards Hamburg.

Of course the crews who flew out night after night on those forty-three major raids (many of them in the Ruhr) between March 5th and July 12th did not know that they had taken part in what historians of the air war called the 'Battle of the Ruhr'. And yet, after the quiet eight weeks of the start of the year, and after the conversion to Lancasters, twenty-five aircraft had failed to return to Warboys between March 5th and July 12th. The squadron had had to renew itself completely, so that new men were coming into Warboys all the time. Something of the calibre of the replacements and new postings has been touched upon earlier in this chapter. F/L Vincent had come in May, G/C Collings in June as C.O., with F/L Hall, soon to become Squadron Navigation Officer. Two further brilliant navigators joined the squadron at the same time as Sam Hall, F/L Mulligan and F/L Geoghegan. Both rose to the rank of squadron leader, with D.F.C.s, and survived their Pathfinder tour and the war. Sadly S/L Tony Mulligan was to perish as a passenger on the ill-fated Avro Tudor *Star Tiger*, together with his wife and his father shortly after the war in 1946, when the aircraft plunged into the Atlantic Ocean. In July two young men, who had done a number of operational flights on 101 Squadron, were posted to Warboys, F/S H. F. Slade and F/S F. J. Fry. Fred Slade, an Australian, was destined to fly on throughout the Ruhr, Hamburg and Berlin offensives, taking his total of 'ops' to fifty-eight, with the fifty-eighth and final one in July 1944, a trip to Hamburg, being the most hairy of the lot. S/L H. F. Slade, D.S.O., D.F.C., of Darlinghurst, New South Wales, died in 1962. Fred Slade's other fellow pilot from 101

Squadron, arriving at Warboys on the same day in July, F/S John Fry from Gravesend, perished exactly three months after joining the squadron. Sadly, John Fry's experience, of three months with 156 was the average length of stay on the squadron. It is paralleled by my father's experience and by that of countless aircrew. Fred Slade's experience was the exception, and, for someone joining the squadron in July 1943 to continue operating until July 1944 was unique.

At the beginning of July three crews were posted to Warboys from 12 Squadron, Wickenby, captained by F/L Fawcett, Sgt. Cromarty, and F/O Illingworth. Only F/O Illingworth and his crew were destined to survive. The first two crews were to perish in the early days of January 1944 in those raids to Berlin that were the occasion of the squadron's most severe losses. F/L Fawcett was to live to become one of the most senior pilots on 156 and when he died, on January 2nd, 1944, he was a squadron leader with a D.F.C..

July 1943 saw the Battle of Hamburg: four major raids upon this second city of Germany which was also Europe's largest port. The city was way beyond Oboe range, although the carefully delineated coastline and the winding River Elbe would make good H2S pictures. Hamburg was, in short, an ideal H2S target. Two further innovations helped the bombers at this time. First, the Gee equipment, constantly jammed by the enemy when the aircraft flew over enemy territory, was improved by the addition of a device, which changed the frequency of the Gee equipment, and thus reduced the jamming. More dramatic still was the introduction of a device known as 'Window', strips of black paper, 27 cms long and 2 cms wide, with thin aluminium foil stuck to one side of the strips. Trials had shown, as long ago as early 1942, that the release of enough of these strips from an aircraft in flight would confuse the German ground-based radar which controlled both the night fighters and the flak guns. Such a revolutionary device was a jealously guarded secret. If it were to fall into German hands it could be used against England. However, after an appeal was made to him, the Prime Minister himself agreed that it was now 'time to open the window', and aircraft were equipped with it.

So now for ten nights, beginning with an attack on Hamburg on July 24th, 'Window' was used with great effectiveness. It is estimated that during the six major raids which took place during those ten nights the 'opening of the window' saved between 100 and 130 aircraft from destruction.

The first Hamburg raid was on July 24th and the crews were ready. The Group Commander, A/C Bennett, had visited Warboys and lectured on the 21st to the aircrew. On July 24th twenty-four aircraft were dispatched to Hamburg, and all returned safely. It was obvious to crews that 'Window' was effective. Searchlights were sweeping drunkenly across the sky, and there was none of the usual co-ordination between searchlight and guns. Out of 791 aircraft sent out against Hamburg only twelve failed to return. Hazards, however, remained always for aircraft on 'ops'. When F/L Vincent's Lancaster was coming in to land at Warboys there was a sudden sound of choking over the intercom. The choking noise was from the bomb aimer who had seen another Lancaster come in out of cloud. The impact of this aircraft, which was landing at Wyton – and one of the circuits almost overlapped that of Warboys – ruptured the glycol tank of F/L Vincent's aircraft, shedding all the coolant, and setting the port engine on fire. The captain called to the engineer to switch off the engine, and feather the propeller. By a mistake that was nearly fatal, the engineer closed down the starboard inner engine instead. A yell from Vin Vincent, and the mistake was corrected. Even so, the stricken Lancaster got a red light from Flying Control, as an aircraft which had just landed was still on the main runway. At 500 feet F/L Vincent told Control he was coming in, despite the red. By the time he landed, the aircraft ahead of them had been towed off the runway onto a perimeter track. It was discovered, on inspection, that the spinner of the port outer engine had been penetrated by the lead weight which was attached to one of the twin tails of the other aircraft. How the crew escaped, with an engine on fire, another wrongly feathered, and the other damaged by a piece of lead the size of a large fist, is a miracle. The Wyton aircraft was being flown at the time by the C.O. of 83 Squadron, G/C John Searby, soon to achieve fame as the Master Bomber in the Peenemunde raid in a month's time, and to become a firm friend of Sam Hall after the war, who was, of course, navigator of F/L Vincent's aircraft, and from whom this information is derived. John Searby's aircraft had had the mid-upper gunner's turret crushed. The occupant of the turret had escaped death by a hair's breadth. Since the leather was removed from the top of his helmet with no disturbance even to his hair, you can appreciate just how literally the term 'by a hair's breadth' is being applied. In addition to this the port tail of the Wyton aircraft was smashed off, and yet, with four engines still functioning, the Lancaster made a good landing, even with half a tail.

It was small wonder that many aircrew developed their own brand of fatalism. And yet, as Sam Hall says, there was no noticeable trauma suffered by any crew member. Nor did they seek to join with the Wyton crew and toast, with heartfelt relief, their mutual and collective good fortune. Three nights later it was business as usual, and another attack on Hamburg. The nearness to instant death, and the fragility of life were routine concomitants of life on an operational Pathfinder squadron.

The second raid on Hamburg on July 27th by 787 bombers was a *Parramatta* attack, an attack using primary blind marking by H2S aircraft. Although the ingredients of this raid were the same as a normal attack on, let us say, Berlin, or a Ruhr city, an unusual combination of weather conditions (high temperature, exceptional low humidity, and dry ground conditions due to lack of rain) produced a firestorm, causing the deaths of many thousands of people. Subsequently thousands evacuated the city, as more attacks were expected and feared. Two crews failed to return to Warboys, out of the eighteen which had set out, those captained by F/O Crompton, and F/S Williams. Although

'Window' continued to be used, nightfighters were there in the bomber stream, and seventeen R.A.F. aircraft were missing from the raid. On July 29th a third Hamburg attack, another one by H2S, took place. This attack was made by 777 bombers, and twenty-three were missing from the attack, among them the Lancaster of F/L B. F. Smith, D.F.C. and F/S Hall, both from Warboys, the last crew being on their first operational flight.

The next night was a 'scrub', and the following night (July 31st) a 'scrub' with every crew at Warboys and other aerodromes involved sitting in their aircraft, and waiting for the green (light) to signal take-off. These 'scrubs' played havoc with the nerves of aircrew, although during the bad weather nights of the Battle of Berlin, later in the year, a different attitude prevailed, and the crews were glad of any respite. In between the first and second Hamburg attacks, on July 25th, Essen was raided, and F/O Hudson and his crew were missing from the thirteen aircraft sent out from Warboys. By day, on July 25th and 26th Hamburg had been attacked in force by the American Eighth Air Force, making the Battle of Hamburg truly a 'round the clock' affair.

The next month, August, proved the busiest month for Bomber Command for the whole of 1943. It began with a fourth Hamburg attack, on August 2nd, the last of the 'Battle of Hamburg', during which all twenty-one Lancasters from Warboys went out and returned, and it developed with a systematic attack on Italian targets on August 7th (Milan, Turin and Genoa) and on August 12th (Turin) and August 15th (Milan). This blitz on Italian cities was an important factor in persuading the Italian government to negotiate an armistice. All the Warboys aircraft who took part in the Italian raids returned safely. The same was true of earlier raids on Mannheim (August 9th) and on Nuremberg (August 10th) and, remarkably, of the raid on the German experimental rocket station at Peenemunde on the Baltic on August 17th. This was a most successful raid, which helped to set back research and development in the V-2 rocket programme. A great deal depended on the Pathfinders for its precise execution. G/C John Searby, the C.O. of 83 Squadron (who had collided with Sam Hall's aircraft when they were about to land after the first Hamburg raid) controlled the attack, on what was, after all, an historic occasion, the first Master Bomber controlling a large Bomber Command raid. And it was complicated. There were three aiming points, and a plan, devised among Pathfinders, for selected crews ('shifters', another choice addition to the Pathfinder vocabulary) to move the marking from one part of the target to another, as the raid went on.

On the Peenemunde raid W/C John White of 156 Squadron, a flight commander on the squadron, acted as the second Deputy Master Bomber, with the C.O. of 405 Squadron, W/C. John Fauquier, acting as the first Deputy. John White played a crucial role in the raid in dropping his markers over the correct point, just when the other marking began to go astray, thus ensuring the bombing, on such a precise target, was on track. Sadly, W/C John White and his experienced crew were killed on the first raid of the Berlin offensive, on November 10th, three months after Peenemunde.

Timing was of the essence during the Peenemunde raid. Sam Hall, flying with F/L Vincent, writes that the role of his aircraft and others on the squadron was to open the final phase of the attack. When his aircraft, therefore, arrived at Ruden Island, four miles away from the target, at one minute earlier than briefed, the pilot responded to the navigator's instruction, 'a one minute turn', by hurling the Lancaster through a 360 degree turn. The crew, of course, tried not to think too much about the armada of aircraft behind them.

When the target was seen by the bomb-aimer, he began to direct Vin Vincent, - 'Steady, steady, left, left'. Sam Hall peered out of his blacked-out navigator's compartment to see how the war was progressing, only to observe a night fighter under the nose of their Lancaster so close to them that the black circles could be seen on the underside of the fighter's wings. The 360 degree turn no doubt saved them from being hit, as the German fighter, having set out on his curve of pursuit, expected them to be ahead by about four miles. Sam drew back the curtains, and turned to his navigation table. In a moment the mid-upper gunner yelled out, 'There's a fighter coming in. He's got a Lanc. – and another – and another.' In a matter of seconds one German fighter had sent three Lancasters to earth in flames.

It had to be agreed that this was, despite the success of the bombing, a good nightfighter night. For the first two phases of the attack a 'spoof' raid on Berlin by Mosquitoes had effectively diverted the German fighters. For the third phase the fighters were there in force, and they accounted for most of the forty bombers missing that night. Warboys, as already indicated, lost none that night, out of the twenty-one dispatched. John Searby received an immediate D.S.O. for his part in the raid. When he landed at Wyton he was still soaked in perspiration.

A few days after Peenemunde there was a raid on Leverkusen during which twelve Warboys Lancasters operated and returned safely. On August 23rd Berlin was raided, the first time since the end of March. It was a large attack, 727 aircraft, and it took its toll, with fifty-six aircraft missing, which was, to date, Bomber Command's greatest loss in a single night. The C. in C. was certainly serious about proceeding from the Ruhr towns and Hamburg to concentrate on Berlin, and some historians, Martin Middlebrook among them (see *The Berlin Raids*, Harmondsworth 1988, p.29ff), consider this raid to be the opening one. It was evident, after the raid, that the Pathfinders had not been able to identify the centre of the 'Big City' with their H2S sets, marking instead an area to the south, on the approaches to the city. P/O Illius and his crew were in the single Warboys Lancaster that failed to return that night. He and his crew had only been posted to Warboys a fortnight before. They were not, however, the only Warboys casualties that night. While over the target, the Lancaster captained by F/S Stevens was hit by flak in the port wing, and at the same time was raked by cannon fire by enemy fighters. The rear gunner, Sgt. Attree, was killed, the aircraft seriously damaged, and the navigator, Sgt. Clegg, and the mid-upper gunner, Sgt. Wright, wounded. The pilot finally, by a superb feat of airmanship, brought the crippled Lancaster in to a landing at Attlebridge.

This first Berlin raid, along the road to the new offensive, whether or not one includes it in the series of raids known as the 'Battle of Berlin' (which forms the theme of a later chapter), was a typical and accurate foreshadowing of the losses Pathfinder crews would suffer, when once the Berlin offensive began in earnest later that year. As it was, the aircraft missing that night included in their aircrew two Pathfinder Station Commanders, G/C B. V. Robinson of Graveley, and G/C A. H. Willetts of Oakington. The flak and the fighters were no respectors of persons. G/C Willetts and the crew with which he was flying became P.O.W.s while G/C B. V. Robinson and all the 35 Squadron crew with whom he was flying perished. Another distinguished Pathfinder pilot who died on this night, and who is referred to in the considerable literature on Pathfinders, was F/L Brian Slade, D.F.C. of 83 Squadron at Wyton, a voluble Londoner, and a real 83 Squadron personality, much loved by his ground crew, by the W.A.A.Fs, and his peers and who was blown up at the start of his bomb run on his fifty-ninth operation. He had aimed to do the double Pathfinder tour of sixty 'ops', and nearly achieved it. The Berlin War Cemetery register states that Brian Slade was only 19, although other sources put him at 21, or 22. He was known at Wyton as 'the boy Slade'. There was another famous Slade in Pathfinders, S/L H. F. (Fred) Slade, who joined 156 Squadron a month before this Berlin raid. He, as already mentioned, did 58 'ops', and left 156 Squadron as S/L H. F. Slade, D.S.O., D.F.C., and died in August 1962 back in his native Australia, aged 49.

The next Berlin raid came at the very end of the month, August 31st. It was, once again, a heavy loss night for the Command as a whole, with forty-seven aircraft missing. And yet, none were from Warboys, although F/O J. L. Wright's Lancaster was attacked by a German fighter over the target. The rear gunner, P/O Crankshaw, gave the fighter a few bursts, and there were reports of the aircraft going into a steep dive, followed by an explosion on the ground. This was, remarkably, a repeat performance. On the previous Berlin raid (August 23rd) F/O Wright's aircraft had been attacked, in the vicinity of the target, by a JU88, and P/O Crankshaw had dispatched it with two bursts of accurate fire. The crew had then witnessed an explosion on the ground, shortly after the JU88 dived to earth. F/O Wright was destined to finish his tour on 156, and his rear gunner with him, F/O K. A. Crankshaw, D.F.M., who, not unnaturally, had attracted a reputation as one of the squadron's most formidable gunners. For these exploits the rear gunner, who, like the pilot, was a New Zealander, was subsequently awarded the D.F.C.

It is time now to turn from this sobering record of sorties and losses during the Ruhr and Hamburg battles, and visit once more the aerodrome itself, and ask ourselves what it was really like when 'ops' were on for both aircrew, ground crew, and all personnel. Woven into this account will be mention of the period immediately after these first renewed attacks on Berlin, in August 1943, the period from September 1943 through to the time when the 'Battle of Berlin' begins in earnest in November. For, although this period was a kind of watershed, crews still went out to heavily defended targets, and losses were still incurred. For Bomber Command, and for the Pathfinders in particular, there was not to be much respite. There were no rest periods, unless it were a stand down for a few days. You prepared for a major bombing offensive against a target or group of targets by operating, and even during the offensive itself you went on operating against targets outside your main area of concentration. For it would not do to have every flak gun in the Reich concentrated on the Ruhr, or Hamburg, or Berlin. The enemy must be kept guessing.

Control tower at Warboys prior to demolition.   *(Taff Jones)*

CHAPTER 5

LIVING AND LOSING

*'You're too young to know what life's all about, but
you're not too young to die.'*

From a speech to aircrew recruits

We last left the crews at R.A.F. Warboys in the crew room at 'Morning Prayers'.
If there were no 'ops' on that night the flight training went on, and flight
commanders dealt with the schedule for the day. Sometimes section leaders,
viz., the Squadron Navigation Officer, Squadron Bombing Leader or Squadron
Gunnery Officer, would have something up their sleeve for aircrew members
in their category, when once the training flights were ended. Often, however,
it was not clear whether 'ops' would be on, or whether the news from 8 Group
Headquarters, who would depend on receiving the word from Bomber Command Headquarters, High Wycombe, was going to come through before lunch.
On days like this men hung around the flight offices to get the 'gen'. Eventually
the word would be given first by means of a telephone call, followed up shortly
by a message on the teleprinter in one of the offices in the Operations Room.
The message told the details of the target, the number of aircraft, bombs and
flares carried, the type of attack, routes, navigational details, and so on. Take-
off time was established, based on E.T.A. on target, and everything else was
worked back from that moment, night-flying test, pilots' and navigators'
briefing (including possibly bomb-aimers, set operators and the like), main
briefing and operational meal. There was not much time, there was never
enough time when 'ops' were on. And yet everything went like a well-oiled
machine, as was natural for a procedure which took place several times a week.
At later times in the war, when Upwood was the airfield and preparations were
being made for daylight raids, there were frantic scrambles to prepare aircraft,
and aircrew had to be wakened at strange hours of the early morning to be ready
for a briefing and a take-off and an arrival over the target which would coincide
in a tactical sense with something happening on the ground, involving the plans
and dispositions of allied troops and their advance. Aircraft, of course, were out
on their dispersals. The hangars at Warboys, three of them, were not used to
house the aircraft so much as for repair.

Warboys aerodrome had three tarmac runways, which looked, from the air, like an inverted triangle, slightly tilted, with the base to the north of the airfield, near to the houses of the village and to St. Mary Magdalene church. Encircling the runways was a perimeter track, narrow enough at fifty feet or so it seemed, to crews in the middle of a taxiing procession of Lancasters. Sprouting off the perimeter track like so many polyps were the dispersals, twenty of them shaped like frying pans, and eighteen of them larger and of a rhombus pattern. The flight offices over which the flight commanders presided were near the Headquarters Building and the 'Ops' Block. When Warboys became a Lancaster squadron there were three flights, A, B and C. By the time the move to Upwood came, it was not long before the squadron was re-formed on the basis of two flights, when 'C' flight moved off to make up 582 Squadron at Little Staughton, together with another flight from Oakington. For most of the time at Warboys there were as many Lancasters as letters of the alphabet, and to flying control, ground crews and their aircrew aircraft were known by their coded letter painted on the side of their fuselage, A to Z, A for Apple through to Z for Zebra. On the side of the fuselage of every Lancaster would be painted the squadron coding, GT, and, following this, A or B, or whatever letter the aircraft was. An aircraft with its particular letter was specially loved by its crew and when the time came to fly another aircraft, due to A for Apple's or Z for Zebra's unserviceable condition, this was not liked. A particular Lancaster was only lucky for its crew. Inevitably, however, there were quite a few changes of crew, and generally, as this or that aircraft disappeared and failed to come back, there was no special feeling about a particular letter, until, that is, another crew had arrived, taken possession of a Lancaster on the squadron, and had flown enough 'ops' to get attached to it.

In reality the aircraft belonged to the ground crew. When 'ops' were on, there they were, over by the dispersal, working many hours to get the aircraft ready for the crew and their next trip. In charge of a team of ground crew was a flight sergeant, usually an older man, and an R.A.F. regular, who had seen some service pre-war. Under him, and in his charge were two sergeants, four corporals, two engine fitters, and two riggers. In addition there were two or three miscellaneous personnel, like electricians, for example, who went from aircraft to aircraft bestowing their particular skill. Such a team, attached to a particular 'flight', would look after two aircraft. Every aircraft, therefore, had its group of individual ground crew, and every morning they worked hard to get their Lancaster ready for the D.I., the Daily Inspection. If it had come in the night before, or in the small hours of the morning damaged and riddled with cannon fire, then the ground crew would start work at once. Those on duty slept in a makeshift hut out by the dispersals where they were most accessible to their aircraft. It was often bitterly cold, and the fitters and riggers and other ground crew often made do with very little sleep. The mobile N.A.A.F.I. wagon would visit them with tea and wads, or the 'Sally Anne', the mobile Salvation Army canteen, with its proud shield on the side emblazoned with the words 'Serving on All Fronts'. Most of the ground crew were not Halton entrants, and had not been trained pre-war. They were men who could repair things, who were good with machines, and they, quite literally, kept the bomber offensive on its feet.

Inevitably, it was a sad task for the ground crew, meeting the men who flew the bombers, out there at the dispersal before take-off, and waiting for them to come in. Friendships were struck up between aircrew and ground crew. It was quite good 'displacement therapy' for ground crew, to talk with particular friends in aircrew, who were about to climb into their Lancasters, about common interests shared, how Preston North End or Blackpool Town were doing until the war came and limited their activities, Yorkshire fast bowlers, the rearing of racing pigeons. A young Welsh flight mechanic, 'Taff' Jones, working on 156 as a member of ground crew, has never forgotten scenes and conversations like these, or the agony of waiting outside the little huts, while the butts of half-smoked cigarettes piled up at the feet of him and his team, as it became inevitable that their aircraft was not going to come in. There were many, many unspoken goodbyes out there at the dispersals while the aircraft turned round on its pan to join the queue on the perimeter track, and taxi out to the main runways for take off. It was, the contribution of those who worked their guts out to prepare the Lancasters for readiness, supremely valuable work. They had the lives of the crew in their hands. They knew this, and the crews knew this. Good aircrews had good ground crew. Sadly, in a multiplicity of cases, there was hardly any time at all to get to know their passing guests. For those few aircrew who completed a tour, or celebrated a special award of a crew member, ground crew were invited as well to the celebrations in a local pub. After all, they were an integral part of the success being celebrated.

For aircrew flying on 'ops', whenever the battle order went up on the noticeboard outside a room in the 'Ops' Block, the precise timetable would unfold. The N.F.T. (Night Flying Test) would take place, at, say, 11.15a.m, a flight of about thirty to forty-five minutes duration during which the pilot ran through his paces with flaps, throttles, and a variety of manoeuvres, while the engineer watched the gauges, the bomb aimer tested his bomb sight, the navigator tested the ever increasing gadgetry his compartment was accommodating, the Gee equipment, the H2S set, and the rest, the W/Op sent out a number of test signals, which were inevitably picked up by the enemy, and used to calculate the strength of the raid they knew would surely come that night, and for which they had to be ready. In addition to those crew members and their responsibilities, the gunners would sit in their turrets and swing their Browning machine guns, and, when at sufficient height, and in a necessary envelope of remoteness, would fire off test bursts. Of course, the perspex of both turrets occupied by the gunners and of the front turrets too, would have been polished enthusiastically by one of the ground crew personnel before the N.F.T. It was no good mistaking that speck or dash of grease for a Junkers 88 or an ME110.

For the first few months of 1943 ground crews got used to a contest between two pilots bringing their Lancasters in to land after their N.F.Ts. They were friends and they were inseparable, a kind of Castor and Pollux among Pathfinder pilots. They were F/L Alastair Lang, D.F.C., and F/L Leighton Verdon-Roe, D.F.C., same rank, same decoration, and they used to compete on their return from N.F.Ts over who could do the tightest turn around the perimeter track with their Lancasters, like two Homeric heroes, racing their chariots before the battle. With a screech of brakes and a smell of scorched rubber from the wheels such Lancaster N.F.Ts certainly demonstrated the skill of the pilots and the versatility of the aircraft. Inevitably the contest did not outlast that other contest with the mounting losses of the time. F/L Lang, one of the contestants, went missing over Dortmund on the night of May 4/5th, while F/L Verdon-Roe died over Duisburg eight nights later, on the night of May 12/13th. F/L Lang survived to become a P.O.W., with two other members of his crew. The other contestant, F/L Verdon-Roe, perished with all his crew. He was a member of the family of that A. V. Roe, whose company produced the Lancaster. There is a sad note, but one which does justice to these two friends and rivals in the Operations Record Book

'F/L Lang, D.F.C., and F/L Verdon-Roe, D.F.C., (both missing) appointed to rank of A/S/L w.e.f. 12th April 1943.'

On the ground Leighton Verdon-Roe used to demonstrate his prowess on his motorcycle, a Harley-Davidson. One night, after a birthday celebration at the Pelican, he rode his motorcycle back from Warboys village and into and through the Officers' Mess, a memorable way of marking what turned out to be his last birthday on earth.

When all the aircraft had come in after their N.F.Ts the bomb dump over on the western side of the airfield, west of the perimeter track, and far away from the main road, was alive with airmen. Bombs were being brought out, having been fused, and placed carefully upon the trolleys, W.A.A.F. drivers were slowly but deliberately driving the linked trolleys out to the aircraft on the hardstanding, where of course these selfsame aircraft were swarming with more personnel, armourers seeing to the guns, or carefully threading the snake-like web of ammunition into the guns and out along the feeder tracks within the Lancasters. The engine cowlings had been removed, engines were stripped down, wherever they had been giving an uncertain signal during the N.F.T., and every effort was being made to place the aircraft in readiness for the night's operation. When the petrol bowsers came to fill up the aircraft, the old hands knew roughly, because of the fuel load, the area of Germany being targeted that night.

Navigators and second navigators operating the H2S sets, the 'Y' equipment, would be given an early operational meal and their own briefing. This was often with their pilots. The complexities of the route, and the details of the marking could then be worked out well in advance of the main briefing, and navigators could make a start on their flight plans. At whatever time these happened, a 7.00pm. take-off time, let us say, augured an operational meal for all aircrew flying on the raid at about 3.15pm., with the main briefing one hour later, and crews out to the aircraft at 6.00p.m. for take-off one hour afterwards.

Individuals, even to-day, can recall particular briefings, the Nuremberg raid in March 1944 when W/C Scott, one of the flight commanders, said that gunners must keep their eyes peeled, as the bright moon made it a good 'nightfighter night', W/C Eaton's last briefing in April 1944, when he disappeared over Friedrichshafen, or W/C Falconer's in December of that same year when he made his last sortie to Cologne. The briefing room's focus in the 'Ops' Block was the enormous wall map of Europe with thin strands of wool extended from Warboys or Upwood across hostile Europe to the target, with pins stuck in the chart deflecting the wool (and hence the progress of the bombers) along this or that track, or dog-leg, to avoid well-defended areas of heavy flak. There were charts unrolled there on the table. Navigators, having had their earlier briefing, were still busy with their flight plans. The intelligence officer would initiate proceedings, after the crews had all entered, the chatter would cease and the briefing would begin.

Meanwhile the sound of the telex could still be heard elsewhere in the 'Ops' Block, and W.A.A.F. clerks would come in, salute smartly, and hand to the C.O. those last minute orders. When the crews entered, the wall map might be veiled, to be swept aside and revealed by way of a dramatic gesture before the start. At other times it was uncovered. After a short spech about the target and its importance from the intelligence officer, the section leaders, beginning with the navigation leader, had their say, giving the information, the 'gen' which their men needed. 'Met', the information about the weather, especially over the target, and, on their return to home airfields, was listened to, with one or two wry comments from an audience all too familiar, from previous trips, with the fact that 'Met' had got it wrong again. The C.O. ended the briefing, wished the crews 'Good Luck' and the men walked out to prepare themselves, to complete flight plans, to go to the Mess for a meal. The meal could often occur after briefing, depending on the time of year, type of target, and, above all, the time when news came through from Group that 'ops' were on that night.

The time of waiting was the worst part. Some aircrew had a last letter, written a while before, left with a friend, who was not on operations, to post to loved ones. Others did not write one. There are photographs of aircrew before a raid in a mess ante-room, sitting in quite comfortable armchairs, turning over the pages of *Flight* magazine, or *Picture Post*, or reading the exploits of 'Jane' in *The Daily Mirror* (the camera angle of the photograph suggests that this is very 'stage-managed'). The operational meal in the Mess, whether eaten before or after the briefing, of bacon and eggs, is a subdued affair.

Dressing for the raid in the locker room had its own ritual significance, as the men climbed into their long underwear, their white operational sweaters,

THU?

as the gunners fastened on their heated suits, and all zipped on their fleece-lined flying boots. Crews had their own private jokes. Tony Toyn, flight engineer at a later stage, in S/L Jack Cuthill's crew, would squeak out his Popeye imitations. A wait for the Bedford transports to arrive to take crews out to dispersals might be enlivened by a particular record on the turntable of a gramophone played in the crew room before the transports came, 'How deep is the night', 'Mrs. Jones, are you coming to bed?', or (slightly inappropriately, you might think) 'I don't want to set the world on fire'. The visit to the parachute section, after they had all dressed, allowed individual aircrew to make that same (lucky) comment to Mavis, the parachute packer, which always raised a smile, 'Can I bring it back, if it doesn't work?'

The men were bulky, in all that clothing, and waddled slightly, as they made their way to the transports. The straps on their parachute harness reached over the shoulders, around their waists and between their legs, while the parachutes themselves were carried, with every man taking great care not to use the ring in the middle of the chute pack as a handle. In the summer months they sprawled on the grass in the open, waiting for the transports, eating fruit from the local orchards or those well remembered strawberries from the fruit farms of Wisbech, not too far from the Wash which they might soon be flying over.

The preparations for the raid had been totally absorbing, and the waiting period, if uncomfortable, was a necessary sequel to efficient preparation. Meanwhile out in the open the ground crew were still working at full pitch. Often, in the days when there were three flights at Warboys, twenty-four aircraft, a 'maximum effort', were detailed for 'ops'; and then, maybe, two or three just could not be made serviceable. A worried flight engineer would speak to his ground crew, the 'Chiefie', the flight sergeant in charge, would shake his head, the flight engineer would speak to his pilot and his section leader, the engineer officer, who, in turn, would inform the C.O., possibly just after the main briefing, and another Lancaster would be allocated (despite the fact that it was only 'lucky' for the crew now on leave), or, if not, that crew would not go on the raid. The flight commanders in particular sought to make available as many aircraft from their flights as they had been asked for, and there was a lot of pressure in various directions to ensure this.

Every crew in every aircraft would learn what their part was in the forthcoming raid and here is where the exotic Pathfinder vocabulary comes in, giving every crew its strict place in the pecking order, giving every pilot, and navigator and set-operator a time, an exact time prior to H-hour, to do their bit, and fulfil their role in Pathfinder H.Q.'s scheme of things. To guide the main force some Pathfinder aircraft dropped flares to mark the route to the target, usually at vital turning points. About fifteen miles from the target an important 'land-marker' would be dropped, to give main force a timed run in on the target. In that way dummy T.Is, planted by the enemy, could be distinguished from the real thing.

Ahead of the marker crews in Pathfinders certain aircraft flew on ahead, pushing out 'Window', those metal aluminium strips which confused and confounded the radar-predicted flak batteries, and which diverted the defences away from the marker aircraft whose job it was to come in straight and level, with no wavering.

When you first joined a Pathfinder squadron you flew a number of trips, as a 'Supporter'. The Supporters only carried H.E. bombs, and they flew in the first wave of aircraft to saturate the defences, and take the flak off the next wave, the Illuminators. These would drop T.Is, short sticks of flares, on the aiming point to light it up. Last of all the Primary Markers arrived over the target, marking the aiming point, already lit up by the Illuminators. Of course there were variations in these roles and tasks. 'Blind Illuminators' dropped their flares after using the H2S set to find their way. 'Blind Markers' marked the target, using their T.Is and skymarkers, only by means of their H2S sets. If, as frequently happened in the early stages, especially for Warboys crews in the June 1943 period, the H2S sets were either unserviceable, or did not work well, those crews simply brought their markers back. 'Primary Visual Markers' identified the aiming point visually, if that was possible, and, if the attack had been planned in that way, using their Mark XIV bombsight, and something called the Group Position Indicator (G.P.I). The navigator fed into the G.P.I. (which was an attachment on the Air Position Indicator) the latest wind speed, and, through adjusting the instrument, obtained not only the air position but also the aircraft's track. That meant that you could make an accurate run by dead reckoning to the target, and could avoid the errors you might otherwise be prone to through having to take violent evasive action, just before you made your run up, from a pre-determined point, to the target.

The 'gen' crews were given the job, usually, of Primary Visual Markers, although there were some crews so good at their job that they never moved from it. 'Supporters', however, never stayed as 'Supporters'. They were always the probationers, the newcomers on a Pathfinder squadron. To the 'old lags' they were the 'cannon fodder', although this nickname was applied with the same wry sympathy as that used by aircrew who called the C. in C. 'Butch' Harris, or just 'Butcher'.

In the final wave of aircraft there came the 'Backers-Up' or 'Visual Centerers'. Their job was to estimate the Mean Point of Impact (the M.P.I.) of the T.Is of the Primary Markers, and drop their target indicators on that centre spot. They had a different colour T.I. from those Primary Markers who had preceded them. If the raid was led, as several of the raids were, from the time of the Battle of the Ruhr onwards the colours were coded and succeeded one another in a *tableau vivant* like the modern traffic indicators: the Mosquitoes, for example, might mark with red, the Primary Markers with yellow, while the Backers-Up used green.

Controlling the raid throughout, and instructing the main force where to bomb, you might hear the calm and steady voice of the Master Bomber, or his

Deputy. In the immediate post-invasion period onwards, Master Bombers and Deputy Master Bombers for many of the raids on transport, railway, and flying bomb and bomb storage sites, and (as the war went on) on major night raids on German cities, were provided by experienced Pathfinder crews from 156 Squadron. Sadly this dangerous work took its toll. Circling the target while the raid was in progress, at a low level, vulnerable to bombs falling from above, and flak from below, the job of being a Master Bomber or a Deputy Master Bomber was not one which actually held out good Life Insurance prospects. You could say this about Pathfinders as a whole but the job of Master and Deputy was one of the most hazardous. The idea of such a closely directed raid had originated with W/C Guy Gibson's controlling actions during the Dams Raid in May 1943, and was, so to speak, pioneered by G/C John Searby who was Master Bomber on the Peenemunde raid in August of the same year. Calm English voices over the R.T. directing operations, like Richard Dimbleby's voice over Berlin in one of those celebrated broadcasts, was a tonic to crews, although Australian, Canadian, and New Zealand voices offered their own special note of vigour and variety.

The type of attack, in terms of method of target marking, varied with the weather, and Bomber Command H.Q. identified the nature of the attack in the signal sent out in accordance with weather conditions, and the Met. advice available. The name of one type of attack, *Newhaven,* was based on the home town of the W.A.A.F. orderly who worked in the Group Commander's Headquarters. This was a visual attack, with crews using their bombsights. If there was haze or cloud over the target of a certain thickness then it would be a *Parramatta* attack, after the Group Commander's birthplace west of Sidney. This meant that the aiming point had to be marked entirely by H2S. If the cloud was impenetrably thick, then the marking was by *Wanganui* flares, flares attached to small parachutes, which often, unfortunately, tended to drift, rendering *Wanganui* the least accurate method.

The H2S sets, being fitted to 156 aircraft in May and June 1943, mid-way through the Battle of the Ruhr showed on the cathode ray tube in the navigator's compartment a series of signals from a receiver fitted in the ventral position, under the belly of the aircraft. The signals formed themselves into a picture giving an outline of the ground beneath, and the outlines, and in some cases other special details of coastlines, rivers and cities could be distinguished. As has already been mentioned, as there were no stabilised aerials in the early sets, you had to fly dead level, not always possible in the heat of combat.

Individuals who had done a certain number of trips on Pathfinders, beginning with, say, six 'ops' as Supporters, and who had performed well in their assigned roles, were awarded the Pathfinder eagle, a silver eagle to be worn on the lapel just below the wing or wings. This eagle was only temporarily awarded, until the Pathfinder aircrew member had done his tour of forty-five operations (including in this any 'ops' flown with another squadron before joining

Pathfinders). It is amazing, in the circumstances, how many Pathfinders came back, after a period of leave to push up their forty-five 'ops' to the fabled sixty. It is equally amazing how many young men embraced with youthful enthusiasm this highly dangerous life. In the narrative, 'historical' sections of this volume it is stated, where it is appropriate to underline it, that the average period of stay for a member of aircrew at Warboys (or, later on, at Upwood) during the twelve months from the start of the Battle of the Ruhr in March 1943 to the end of the Battle of Berlin in March 1944 was only three months.

These circumstances and responsibilities and structured destinies faced these young men, who climbed into the transports to be taken out to the dispersals quite often by a cheerful W.A.A.F. driver to chat with their ground crew, and to wait, yet again. Always the waiting. The pilot of the aircraft would be given Form 700 to sign by a member of ground crew, signing over the aircraft to him, now that it had been pronounced serviceable. There were, inevitably, the mascots, the rag doll, a little bit worse for wear, who had been on many trips, and (so the pilot assured anyone who would listen) suffered from high altitude. One man insisted on going on 'ops' with a walking stick, gunners draped their Brownings in St. Christopher medals, or, in more earthy fashion, with appropriate items of female underwear. W.A.A.Fs' 'passion killers', black pants that were good for polishing perspex were a special favourite in this context. Men wore girlfriends' stockings wrapped around their necks, pilots, navigators, W/Ops and engineers stuck pictures of wives, children, girlfriends at appropriate points in their own special sections or compartments of the aircraft. Sam Hall once decided he would not speculate any more, on putting his hat in the locker on top of his clothes, before an 'op', on whether he would see that hat again. He took it with him, and his crew, whichever crew he was flying with, would not let him go off without it. Some crews, or individuals in crews, said prayers, out there beside the aircraft, others 'christened' the tail wheel of the Lanc. before climbing in, others touched for luck in the Bedford truck a particularly 'lucky' aircrew member, probably not from your own crew, but from a crew of the same flight.

There were aircrew, who, in the midst of such a dangerous and highly technical life, took quite seriously the existence of 'chop girls', those girls, usually members of the squadron, W.A.A.Fs or other personnel, who had been out with a number of aircrew, every one of whom had 'got the chop' in succession. These poor girls were shunned, and there were, inevitably, quite a number of them on an operational Pathfinder station. Superstitions flourished in the midst of such fearful odds, and the fact that this was a war of machinery seemed to encourage rather than diminish these manifestations. After all, in aircrew parlance, they were all 'dicing' that night.

There was very little 'nose art' on Lancasters of a Pathfinder squadron, apart from the bombs routinely painted, in contrast to what you found, say, on the B17s of the American Eighth Air Force, flying from nearby Alconbury, where the Wellingtons of 156 main force squadron used to be housed in the early months of 1942. Australians liked their bombers with symbols and pictures painted on the nose, such as 'Kelly's Gang Rides Again', and pictures of a reclining *Jane* from the pages of the *Daily Mirror*. But this was confined to R.A.A.F. Squadrons, such as 462 and 466 Squadrons at Driffield with their Halifaxes, and to the Lancasters of 460 Squadron at Binbrook. One popular Australian character on 156 Squadron, however, short, and extrovert, and full of fun, who was for a time in S/L Walbourne's crew, and who rejoiced in the name of Love (W/O, later P/O, and with a D.F.C), had painted 'Love will find a way' around his guns in the rear turret.

There would usually be quite a crowd of station personnel waiting along the perimeter track, or near the control tower by the take off runway to wave at the aircraft when they set out. Crews would be there at their individual stations and positions in the aircraft looking for the green signal given by one of the control personnel. Previously they had all gone through their own drills. Navigators had laid out charts, pencils, calculators, sextants, pilots had run through a cockpit drill, with flight engineers checking gauges and dials. Bomb aimers had gone down into the nose to check the settings of the bombs, the switches on the bombsights, and the camera. Wireless operators were bent over their sets, as were the Spec. Navigators, if the aircraft carried them. Gunners were swinging their power driven turrets, and checking their guns. As the time for take-off drew near, the ground crew plugged in the 'trolley ack' (that is, the battery cart), the engines, Rolls Royce Merlins, chattered into life, like the crack of pistol shots. When the 'green' came, the green light from the control tower, it was off, 'Good luck, skipper', and thumbs up from the ground crew, individual salutations and encouragements for crew members, and out of the dispersal pan or hard standing, to join the queue on the perimeter track, and then away. The crews departing from Warboys made the windows rattle in the church of St. Mary Magdalene at the northern end of the airfield.

Near the cemetery just beyond St. Mary Magdalene church and at the southern end of the village of Warboys the road that led out of the village was blocked by a barrier, since the main runway of the airfield crossed it. A newly married navigator had 'hidden' his bride in Warboys village, contrary to the regulation that wives must not live near a front line operational station. The navigator (this was in the mid-June 1943 period) finished his tour and left Warboys, taking with him his bride, who, every time her husband was on 'ops', could be seen, standing there by the barrier, waving to her husband, while he waved back from the astrodrome on take off, rather like Lucasta in a bygone age waving off her chevalier going to the war. Others would be gathered there by the same barrier. Indeed the way to the airfield, past the church and cemetery to the barrier, became a favourite walk, and crews used to wave to children and well wishers, while they took off on their N.F.Ts, while the ground crew who serviced the aircraft were often overlooked by little knots of gazing children.

The alternative road, built by the R.A.F. to bypass the airfield and connect Warboys with the road to Huntingdon, was affectionately known as the 'concrete road'. It has helped to shape the road system in and around Warboys village which exists at the present time.

On returning from an operation and coming back to land at Warboys or Upwood a pilot might expect to hear on the R.T. a cool, clear and articulate W.A.A.F.'s voice announcing after the call sign the permission to land. Down comes the undercarriage, the wheels touch on the ground. and the W.A.A.F. is there with the Bedford truck or crew 'bus' and a relieved little knot of ground crew are there to welcome you. 'Good trip, skipper? Any trouble with the kite?' And then with a crash of gears the tired crew, who do not feel like talking very much, are taken by the truck to the Headquarters area to de-briefing and interrogation. There the handed out drink is a steaming mug of tea laced with rum, and the incoming crews flock to individual tables surrounded by chairs. New crews are known to talk a lot about their trip, older crews don't say a lot, but wait to answer the standard questions about the route, the flak, the fighters, the combats, the markers, any aircraft seen going down, the met., any unusual features, and so on. Intelligence officers are usually skilled and patient, and know how to get the best out of returning crews, information which could, of course, prove vital for future journeys back over enemy territory. At Upwood it was then a walk to breakfast in the Mess and another short walk to those neat avenues of houses where the billets were. At Warboys, by contrast, the trucks waited during de-briefing to take aircrew back to the Messes a mile or so away and to the accommodation area. Sam Hall liked to walk this distance, often just as the dawn was breaking, back along the road to Old Hurst and Huntingdon. The stillness after the noise of a Lancaster's engines, the accumulated tensions of a raid draining away, the sight of smoke rising up from the chimney of a thatched cottage (yes – the thatched cottage is still there) all these things soothed and healed and prepared an already weary senior navigator for the benison and boon of sleep. Some could not sleep, but lay on their beds smoking quietly. And meanwhile the casualties, if there were any, were making themselves felt. The ground crew of B for Baker had waited out there in the cold until it was clear that the aircraft had not enough fuel to keep it in the air, it was so long overdue. That W.A.A.F. in the 'Ops' room had waited, like the ground crew, because her fiancé was the W/Op in the missing aircraft. There were, quite often, tears in the W.A.A.Fs' dormitory, heard low, almost supressed, as girlfriends, fiancées, good friends simply, tried hard to conceal and come to terms with the near certainty of the loss of the aircrew in their lives. There was not much time for dramatic expressions of grief. It was bad for morale. People just got on with the job. The next day it may be that there would be 'ops' on again, and the long drama of the preceding twenty-four hours would be played out again. As for aircrew, their feelings, as human beings who had lost close friends, were obvious. Once again, however, there was the powerful, the overwhelming instinct to supress feelings, not to mention the name of the missing in the Mess, or wherever aircrew foregathered. After the Committee of Adjustment had done their work, and dealt with the missing man's effects, it was just as though he had left the squadron, as indeed he very likely had. When they did talk of death, these aircrew, it was in those famous clichés which were to become the raw material of satire in a more lighthearted age, but which were more than adequate to talk about those things you did not want to take in, own, or acknowledge: old so-and-so had 'bought it', or 'gone-for-a-Burton', or in the event of a crash-landing pilot and crew had walked away from, terrifying in its potential for extinguishing lives in an instant, it was simply said that 'Sandy had bent the kite a bit'. Furthermore, an operation was described in terms borrowed from light entertainment: it was a 'good show', especially if the target had been 'clobbered'. You might even say it had been a 'wizard prang'. And perhaps most revealing of all, if a girlfriend finally turned you down, or broke off the relationship, she simply 'shot you down in flames'. Some of these clichés have survived. The most popular of them all is the oftheard expression that so-and-so is 'getting a lot of flak' from some individual or group. But then our country's wars have always enriched and extended our vocabulary, and have furnished a great many of our expressions.

'Going for a Burton', however, was not all that could happen to you if you failed to return from an 'op'. You might be on the run, you might be 'passed down the line' by one of the resistance movements in occupied Europe, or, the most widely feared of all fates, short of meeting death itself, you might, if you baled out over the target area, be left to the tender mercies of the crowd. An aircrew member of a Pathfinder squadron, Alf French, has spoken of how very badly treated he and the survivors of his crew were by the angry local population, when he baled out in the latter months of the war. When you baled out, you were conscious that you might have lost friends (in many cases you knew you had). The combined shock of this loss, and the subsequent nightmare of violent treatment meted out was something which burnt itself deeply into the consciousness of many, many young men. Details like this remind us of how very much we owe these brave men who went on and on, doing their duty.

One great boost or thrill, which helped aircrew to carry on, when the empty chairs at the post-operational meal got to them, or the unoccupied beds in the nissen hut, was the photograph of their marking or bombing performance, taken over the target on release of bombs or markers, which, if it showed an aiming point, or something pretty near it, was a cause for congratulation. Such photographs were pinned up, side by side, for all to see. They were, it must be said, a powerful incentive. Your place in a league table, known as the 'bombing ladder' was important to all members of the crew. The Squadron Bombing Leader would, of course, keep an eye on weak crews.

The Battle of the Ruhr, and the offensive against Hamburg which immediately followed it, was a period of great attrition for the squadron, and a period which actually continued, lasting throughout the early feints on Berlin, and the other targets attacked. A third Berlin raid (after the two that took place in August) was made on the night of September 3rd, 1943. Twenty Lancasters from Warboys visited the capital, one, captained by F/O Shanahan failed to get back, while another aircraft, on a training exercise that day, crashed near East Wretham. The aircraft was piloted by F/O Foderingham, D.F.C., and all the crew were killed, with the exception of the flight engineer. To lose a senior pilot and crew like this, at a time when so many were not returning from night raids, was tragic. And it went on. F/O Prichard and his crew were lost over Mannheim two days after the Berlin raid, while two crews were shot down on a Munich raid the very next night (F/L Machlachlan, D.F.C., and F/O Lutz, D.F.C. with their crews). This amounted to a loss to the squadron of six aircraft in three nights. For a period of six days there was now a stand down from 'ops', with the usual programme of intensive 'Y' training (training with the H2S sets), Bombing and Air Firing flights, Air to sea firing, and low flying. One aircraft contributed to an interesting attack at a Dunlop rubber factory in central France on the night of September 15th. The Master Bomber was W/C D. F. E. C. Deane, D.F.C., who was C.O. of 35 Squadron at Graveley. This was the last occasion on which Pathfinders provided a Master Bomber to direct the main force until the spring of 1944. 'Dixie' Deane of 35 Squadron was often confused with another powerful character, G/C L. C. Deane, D.S.O., D.F.C., who completed a tour with 156 later this year, 1943, and was sent to Wyton to command 83 Squadron on January 3rd 1944 after their C.O., W/C Abercromby, D. F.C. had failed to return early in December.

Towards the end of the month of September the targets continued to be bombed. The Modane railway yards were visited, an important target, on the main route from France to Italy, on September 16th. On September 27th twenty-one aircraft set out for Hannover, and an experienced pilot and crew failed to return. S/L Vincent, D.F.C., was the captain, and he took along as 'second dicky' the newly arrived Sgt. Knight to gain operational experience. The month ended with another crew becoming casualties. Ten aircraft took off for Bochum on September 29th, and one of them, with F/S Ray and his crew, crashed at Downham Market. All the crew were killed, with the exception of the rear gunner, Sgt. Orchard. Early the next month on October 4th S/L Syd Cook, D.F.C., D.F.M., failed to return from a raid on Frankfurt, taking with him as navigator F/O Peter Godfrey. Peter Godfrey was navigator to F/L 'Tiny' Anset. He was standing in for P/O Harry Wright in Syd Cook's crew. Harry, who wrote a novel, *Pathfinders Light the Way* (published in 1983), about his experiences, was sick that night, and could not go. He survived to finish a total of seventy-eight 'ops', nearly fifty of these with Pathfinders.

Syd Cook's loss was keenly felt by former 103 Squadron friends, of whom there were a number on 156, as well as by Harry Wright. Don Charlwood speaks of Syd, an Australian fellow countryman, and of Harry, the survivor, a navigator like himself in that haunting classic of Bomber Command literature, *No Moon Tonight*. Syd Cook had joined the squadron as a flight lieutenant earlier that year in April, not long before the New Zealander, Mandy Mandeno, in the 'old days' (for a week is a long time in Pathfinders) when W/C Rivett-Carnac commanded the squadron. The navigator, Peter Godfrey, who took the place of Harry Wright in Syd Cook's crew, had been a long time with his skipper F/L Tiny Anset. When Peter was missing, Tiny borrowed a light aircraft and flew up north to break the news to Peter's parents, a hard thing for anyone to do, but to Tiny, his task and his tribute to Peter.

Sam Hall, at the same time as Tiny Anset lost his navigator, knew all about grieving and losing. By this time, in the autumn of 1943, he had lost three pilots he had flown with, since coming back on operations, as a navigator, in the middle of the year. In June 1943 he had been posted with G/C Collings from the new Canadian Pathfinder squadron, 405, at Gransden Lodge the other side of Cambridge, where he had flown a number of 'ops' with P/O Mattock, an experienced pilot, who was shot down, and became a P.O.W. shortly after Sam was posted to Warboys. A week after arriving at Warboys he flew with S/L McIntosh, and they decided to crew up, with Sam acting as his navigator. A week later Sam went on leave, and S/L McIntosh went missing. Finally Sam flew fifteen operations with S/L Vincent, (some details of those flights were recounted in the previous chapter), before being pulled out to become Squadron Navigation leader. And, as we have seen, earlier in this chapter, S/L Vin Vincent and his crew failed to return from Hannover on September 27th. Sam Hall was out on the same night over Hannover, flying with the C.O., who saw a Pathfinder aircraft in trouble jettisoning its flares. That night they were diverted to Downham Market, and at breakfast the next morning there was a call to tell the C.O. that Vin and the crew were missing. Later it was established that the blazing Pathfinder aircraft they had seen was most likely theirs.

Back at Warboys Tiny Anset tried to divert Sam Hall and take him out of himself, when he found him brooding alone in a corner of the Mess that evening. Finally he persuaded Sam to come out with the station M.O., Peter Bryce-Curtis, and the Intelligence Officer, who, because of certain facial character-istics and a slight, balding condition, appropriate to that fabled character after whom a humorous magazine is named, rejoiced in the nickname of 'Punch'. At the Pike and Eel, one of the oldest pubs in the land (and still delightful to this day) a few miles out of Warboys, at Holywell on the river Ouse a meal had already been ordered. Sam Hall drank some wine and thought of the aircrew brothers he had lost, for a crew were brothers, thrown together to endure life's extremes, and maybe life's ending. In a small parlour there was a piano, and at this piano, and after the meal, Tiny played and sang for two hours.

This gives me a chance to introduce Tiny, a squadron character of real accomplishment. Tiny had been a cathedral chorister, and, when the war began, was a choral scholar at one of the ancient universities. One night, earlier than the time of this excursion to the Pike and Eel, there had been an E.N.S.A. concert at Warboys. The troupe of performers had adjourned to the Mess and were giving a repeat performance. The C.O., G/C Collings, asked Tiny Anset to help with the entertainment. At the piano Tiny gave a repertoire of such variety that he quite eclipsed the E.N.S.A. team. First, an English folk song, *Buttercup Joe*, in dialect, then the aria from La Bohème, *Che Gelida Manina* (Your tiny hand is frozen), followed, and finally *Ave Maria*, sung in a faultless tenor. You could have heard a pin drop,' recounts Sam Hall, 'as Tiny sang *Ave Maria*, which is no mean achievement at one o'clock in the morning in front of a Mess full of aircrew who have been drinking steadily for two hours.'

That night Tiny had established a precedent, and a reputation. Henceforward, whenever he sat down to play in the Mess, conversation, chatter, noise would die down, and aircrew would wait for Tiny to begin. Tiny was as one born out of due time. Had he survived the war he could have been a Gerard Hoffnung or a Donald Swann, for he loved doing extravagant, clowning impressions at the piano. His masterpiece was an impression of a wild, eccentric, central European pianist, which resulted in his failing to hit the keyboard with the last frenzied chord, so that he pitched off the stool and rolled on the carpet. But, as we have seen, Tiny could command attention by his renditions of serious music no less than by his clowning. His was the true manner of the troubadour, the classic tradition of the one who jokes in earnest. The tears were never far from the surface, but, like all good aircrew, the tears never really fell. The living, the flying, the losing and the grieving were translated into his music. When he lost friends, he played and sang. When others lost friends, he played and sang to them. And side by side with all this, there was Tiny's utter determination to 'press on', this cliché which meant that you never flinched, weaving all the way to the target, but straight and level, straight through the flak with an immaculately steady bomb run, and an aiming point photograph when you returned.

After a welcome period of leave in November, Sam Hall returned to Huntingdon. Peter Bryce-Curtis, the M.O., met him in at the railway station to take him back to the airfield. He often went to do this; but this time he had a special purpose. When Sam asked him what had been happening, the M.O. said two words, 'Tiny's missing', and Sam never said another word as they threaded through Huntingdon, past Wyton, and on the way to Warboys. Sam Hall had watched his friends go, one by one, crew by crew, and now the one who had tried to console him had gone the way the others had taken. Tiny had perished over Berlin on November 22nd, with all his crew. At the time he died, Tiny, the troubadour pianist and singer, the one who could, like a twentieth-century Orpheus, steal away the hearts of the morose, the tense, and the flak-happy, was a squadron leader, with a D.F.C. awarded ten days before. Sam Hall's short piece published in the Winter/Spring 1981 number of *The Marker*, the magazine of the Pathfinder Association, entitled *Remembering a Friend*, from which the details of this episode are taken, is a beautiful, and finely written elegy to those who failed to return to Warboys at this period. It bears comparison with one of H. E. Bates' *Stories of Flying Officer X*, a collection of stories based on the time the author was stationed at Oakington. Speaking of H. E. Bates, it is often the case that those who can write in a richly comic vein (witness the Pop Larkin series of books, now televised) understand and can write about the tears that lie at the heart of things, the grim business of losing, of sustaining losses that was an ineluctable part of life on a Pathfinder station.

Of course there were crews that came through the dark period of the Battles of the Ruhr and of Berlin. F/L Peter Isaacson completed a tour on 156 early in 1943, to be chosen by the Australian government to fly a Lancaster to his home country, Australia, via Canada, the United States, Hawaii, and Fiji. Peter Isaacson's crew were all Australians, and all from 156. The Lancaster they flew was welcomed to great applause when they landed in Queensland at Amberley on June 3rd, 1943. F/L Isaacson has spoken of his experiences of 'living and losing' at Warboys on 156 Squadron in a documentary film made in Australia about Australian airmen and broadcast in the autumn of 1988 in this country, entitled *Wing on the Storm*. His navigator Bob Nielsen, an Australian now living in California, recalls the flight they made in Lancaster ED930 from this country to Australia in a fascinating book, entitled *With The Stars Above*, published in Washington in 1984. Another Australian, S/L Bill Manifold, D.F.C. and Bar, completed a Pathfinder tour on 156 at this period, after an initial tour with 467 R.A.A.F. Squadron at Bottesford. F/L Harold Hernaman, D.F.C. was a W.Op/ A.G. in his crew, and is to be seen at the annual memorial services that are held in St. Mary Magdalene, Warboys, which are great occasions for remembering lost friends and the life of those days, and at which I have had the privilege of being the preacher three times. The crew of S/L Jack Cuthill (now retired and living in his native British Columbia) took in a long Pathfinder tour from the dark January days of 1944 at Warboys to the 'sunlit uplands' of post-invasion days at Upwood. Bob Trotter, the second navigator in the Cuthill crew (F/L Trotter, D.F.C.), has kept the squadron register with skill and efficiency, and his help has been invaluable in my contacting aircrew of the squadron of all periods of the war. Ron Breeze, flight engineer with S/L Cuthill, has written his impressions and memories of the life of those days in a unique diary, which supplements his log book, and which I have made extensive use of. Sadly, Tony Toyn, flight engineer in the same crew, after Ron Breeze finished his tour, died on Christmas Eve, 1991, but his Popeye imitations, while the crew were dressing for a raid, live on. F/L Trevor Timperley, D.F.C., was another pilot, not an Australian, who completed a tour in those critical days of 1943 from the middle of the year until November, after which he was posted to No. 14 O.T.U. He had flown Wellingtons at Kirmington with 166 Squadron before coming to Warboys.

Also posted in November 1943, after completing a tour with 156 was F/L Drew, D.F.C., who proceeded to 24 Squadron in Transport Command. Other successful pilots who 'made it' include W/C Donaldson, D.F.C., posted to command 1637 C.U. in June, 1943, and a New Zealander, F/L R.S.D. Kearns, D.F.C., D.F.M, whose flying days on the squadron dated from the days of the Wellingtons, and there were others. 'Terry' Kearns, Peter Isaacson, Alastair Lang and Leighton Verdon-Roe were referred to by the C.O. of the time, W/C Rivett-Carnac, as the 'fearsome foursome'.

Bill Manifold, the Australian pilot, and Harry Wright, the Australian navigator (in Syd Cook's crew until he went missing), have both gone to their rest recently. Another Australian, W/C 'Digger' Duigan, D.F.C., now deceased, finished during mid 1943 a hectic and adventurous tour, fondly recalled in the *156 Register* by his bomb aimer, F/O 'Dusty' Drake, D.F.C., D.F.M., which included a bale out over Chatteris for the whole crew on May 4th after coming back from Dortmund. W/C Duigan was posted to No. 81 O.T.U. as Chief Instructor in September 1943, after another tour with 156 Sqadron, as the 'A' flight commander. He left with over 100 'ops' to his credit, having succeeded, in addition, in marrying one of the W.A.A.F. officers on the station.

Turning from Australians to New Zealanders, S/L Mandeno, already mentioned in the previous chapter, completed his tour and returned to his native New Zealand, where he still lives in retirement. S/L J. L. Wright, D.S.O., D.F.C., a fellow New Zealander like S/L Mandeno, was posted to Uxbridge in November, 1943, on completion of his operational tour. Another New Zealander, Sam Hall, now G/C H.R. Hall, O.B.E., D.F.C. and domiciled in Belmont, Surrey, has told me much about those 1943 days at Warboys where he was Squadron Navigation Leader, after losing those three pilots and crews he flew with in the manner outlined in this chapter. He was posted to H.Q. Bomber Command, High Wycombe in December 1943. His unpublished memoirs, *Time Flying*, have the authentic flavour and idiom of life on an operational Pathfinder station in 1943. Of particular interest are the tremendous changes that had taken place, since he did his first tour on Wellingtons with 1X Squadron at Honington in 1940.

Of course some members of 156 Squadron not only completed their tours on the squadron but went on to command other squadrons or units within Pathfinders. G/C G. H. Womersley. D.S.O., D.F.C. and Bar was at Warboys from August 1942 as a pilot (W/C) and flight commander until he was posted to the staff of Pathfinder Headquarters in April 1943. For a period in 1944 Geoff Womersley commanded the Mosquito Squadron 139 'Jamaica' Squadron which was based at Upwood, and was part of the Pathfinder Light Night Striking Force, while in February 1945 he became Station Commander at Gransden Lodge. G/CL. C. Deane. D.S.O. D.F.C. was another pilot and flight commander who served with distinction on 156, leaving there as W/C Deane, D.F.C., to be posted to Wyton in January 1944 to command 83 Squadron, after the previous C.O., W/C Abercromby D.F.C., had been killed over Berlin. Another similar pilot, the 'C' flight commander, was a red-haired Canadian, W/C G. F. Grant, D.S.O., D.F.C. He left Warboys in November 1943 on a staff posting to

Headquarters. In May 1944 he was C.O. of 109 Squadron, an Oboe Mosquito marker squadron at Little Staughton, formerly at Wyton, while in December 1944 he became Station Commander of Graveley. W/C W. T. Brooks, O.B.E., D.S.O., A.F.C., the 'A' flight commander, was posted in April 1944 just before the C.O's disappearance over Friederichshafen, to command 635 Squadron, a newly formed Pathfinder squadron at Downham Market, flying Lancasters. In August 1944 W/C W.W.G. Scott, D.F.C. 'B' flight commander on 156, was posted to command 608 Squadron, newly re-formed at Downham Market, and flying Mosquitoes, as part of the Pathfinder Light Night Striking Force.

Early in September 1944 W/C K. J. Burrough D. F.C., 'A' flight commander of 156, was called away from Upwood to Wyton, pending a posting. On September 15th he became C.O. of 128 Squadron, re-formed on that date at Wyton as yet another Mosquito squadron in the rapidly expanding Pathfinder Light Night Striking Force. Nor was 156 Squadron noted only for outstanding pilots, who proceeded, after completing a tour on the squadron, and often after being flight commanders, to command squadrons or even aerodromes. There were some outstanding section leaders on the squadron at this time. W/C Ken Lawson D.F.C. was posted on June 7th 1943 from 156 Squadron to Headquarters 8 Group as Group Navigation Officer. In the last few months of the War Ken Lawson was back on 156 sqadron, having remustered as a pilot. Two navigators reported to Warboys on June 14th 1943 from the N.T.U. at Upwood. They were F/Ls Mulligan and Geoghegan, and both achieved distinction in the squadron. S/L Mulligan, D.F.C. became on May 12th 1944 squadron navigation officer, after flying in W/C Grant's crew, while S/L Geoghegan, D.F.C., after flying in S/L H. F. Slade's crew, was posted to the Pathfinder N.T.U. (now at Warboys) on March 23rd 1944. Both survived some of the worst times in the history of 156. Sadly, Tony Mulligan, as this book relates in the appropriate place, went down as a passenger on the ill-fated *Star Tiger* of British South American Airways in 1946, not long after the war. We have mentioned Sam Hall, who, after being squadron navigation leader in late 1943 was posted to H.Q. Bomber Command on the staff in December. His successor, S/L D.H. Thomas, D.S.O., D.F.M., was posted to H.Q. No. 3 Group on March 1st, 1944, and S/L J. F. Hacking, D.F.C. and Bar took up this post. When he laid it down on May 12th, 1944, S/L Mulligan succeeded. Another squadron navigation officer whose section leader duties relate to a later stage was S/L R. H. Dean, D.F.C., the H2S Leader, whose service with 156 spanned the period from November 1943 until the war's end. F/L Foster, the Squadron Bombing Leader, was attached to H.Q. No. 3 Group for Group Bombing Leader duties in June 1943. In September of that year he was promoted to Squadron Leader and awarded the D.F.C. There were section leaders on 156 who had a different career, like S/L Everson, D.F.C., Squadron Gunnery Leader, who was posted in mid-1943 to the R.A.F. delegation in the U.S.A.

Sadly, other section leaders simply did not survive their time on 156. Two squadron bombing leaders met their end, while serving with 156, S/L Glasspool, D.F.C., on April 23rd, 1944, while flying with W/C Eaton, the C.O., and F/L D.T. Wood, D.F.C. who was acting as visual marker commander, on June 8th, 1944. Two squadron gunnery leaders also died, S/L A. Muir, D.F.C., on February 21st 1944, and S/L J. P. Blair, D.F.C., D.F.M., on May 21st of that year after having done sixty-six 'ops'. Two squadron engineer leaders were also killed in action during their time on 156, F/L Manvell D.F.C., D.F.M. on June 27th 1944 (he had had a good spell on the squadron, having been posted there a year earlier, June 18th 1943, from 1656 C.U)., and F/L W. N. Bingham, who was flying with the C.O., W/C Falconer, on the night of December 30th, 1944. To be a section leader was to be in a dangerous and exposed position. You supervised your own area, and helped to plan the raid, briefing the crews with your own 'gen', and flying with them quite often. Six section leaders is a lot for a squadron to lose in ten months, and testifies to their conscientiousness and sense of duty. Often they would fly with a fairly new pilot and crew to give them confidence. That, sadly, is when several of them met their end. Another career in Pathfinders which required courage of the highest order was that of Master Bomber and Deputy Master Bomber. Their exploits and their casualties are recounted in chapter 7. Some, of course, did come through, but 156 Squadron lost many pilots and crews of the very best kind in terms of courage, ability, and experience, in those calls made upon them, time and again after the invasion, to provide Master and Deputy Master Bomber for a whole range of targets.

There was no lull in operations in the lead up to the Battle of Berlin, and a whole series of operations took place to a number of German cities. Earlier in this chapter the death of S/L Syd Cook, D.F.C., D.F.M., over Frankfurt, was recounted. Following this sad incident (for Syd Cook was one of the squadron's veterans) there were raids on Stuttgart (October 7th), Hannover (October 8th) and a diversionary raid against Bremen, Hannover again on October 18th, Kassel (October 22nd), Dusseldorf (November 3rd), Modane (November 10th), and Mannheim (November 17th). On November 18th came the first in the series of raids against Berlin, to become known, collectively, as 'The Battle of Berlin', which was to take away from the squadron a host of flight commanders and their very senior crews, so that the 8 Group Commander, A/V/M/ Bennett, was to lament that from now until the battle ended at the end of March, the Pathfinder squadrons were to lose one and a half times their own strength.

During the night of October 8th, P/O Fry and his crew went missing. They had been taking part in the diversionary raid of 119 aircraft upon Bremen, while 504 aircraft bombed Hannover. Just after bombing, and after the bomb doors had been closed, John Fry's Lancaster was coned. Flak was pumped up, and two German fighters dived in pursuit. The gunners put up a spirited defence, until the mid-upper gunner could fire no more, as his turret jammed, and the navigator's compartment became a mass of flames. Corkscrewing violently the

Lancaster evaded the fighters, and yet developed a vertical spin. John Fry gripped the controls to pull the Lancaster out of the spin. After dropping like a stone for 6,000 feet he managed to pull the bomber out, and to hold it straight and level, after which he gave the order to abandon aircraft. Two of the four engines were on fire by now, and it was obvious that the aircraft was doomed. Even so P/O Fry stayed at the controls to allow the crew to bale out. F/O Poole, the Canadian navigator in the crew fixed John Fry's parachute for him and called out, 'Come on Johnnie.' With that the Lancaster blew up. F/O Poole dropped to earth at an unhealthy speed. He had suffered burns and there was a large hole in his parachute. Had his fall not been cushioned somewhat by dropping into a muddy, ploughed field, it is doubtful whether he would have lived. Even so he now suffered further extensive injuries, which were so severe that he was repatriated before the end of the war by the Red Cross. Sadly four members of the crew were killed that night, when the bomber blew up, while three, including the navigator, survived. F/O Poole visited John Fry's parents after his repatriation to tell them and his teenage brother Arthur the story of their son's last moments.

There is a sequel to this story. For some inexplicable reason the name of the gallant pilot, P/O F. J. Fry, was omitted from the book in Ely Cathedral containing the names of those who lost their lives while serving with Pathfinders in 8 Group. The other members of his crew who died with him are included in this book; but his name was omitted. Due to the efforts of his brother Arthur, a teenager when John died, and of some members of the Pathfinder Association, the name of P/O F. J. Fry was incorporated into the Roll of Honour, and a special service of dedication conducted by the Dean was held on March 2nd of this year to mark the occasion. Mr. Arthur Fry and his wife were present, and some friends, who knew John, Taff Jones and Norah of 156 Squadron, together with S/L Peter Coggan, D.F.C. and F/L Jimmy Hughes, D.F.M. and Mrs. Hughes. I had the pleasure of being present also. Through this episode and the efforts to have P/O Fry's name included in the book, I received the details of John Fry's story which are included in this narrative. It is a special pleasure to have John's name on the Roll of Honour in Ely before the fiftieth anniversary of the foundation of the Pathfinders which is to be celebrated in a special service in the Cathedral on August 16th of this year. For Ely Cathedral was, of course, a landmark for all Pathfinder crews as they set out for Germany, and, if they were fortunate, returned, just as Lincoln Cathedral was a landmark for 1 and 5 Groups, York Minster and Beverley Minster for 4 Group, and Ripon Cathedral for those Yorkshire-based aircraft of the Canadian 6 Group. John Fry had moved to the squadron on July 8th, as a flight sergeant, together with Fred Slade, the Australian colossus who did 58 'ops', and stayed on the squadron at Warboys, and later Upwood, until August 1944. They had come from 101 Squadron, which had recently moved from the Yorkshire base, Holme-on-Spalding-Moor, to Ludford Magna in Lincolnshire. John was a devout Methodist, whose father was a Methodist Lay Preacher. The Methodist church in Warboys meant a lot to John and his family, as did the friends he met there. Chapels and churches were foremost in encouraging families to open their homes to these young men. John and his friends on the airfield used to cycle into the village during quiet times and stand downs, and gain, in those snatched moments, that genuine hospitality which allowed a young man, weary after the previous night's raid over Berlin, simply to sit and go to sleep on a sofa, or read a newspaper or listen to music, or in short to be a member of the family. There is a lot of quiet pride in these people of Warboys even to-day as they look back with affection on their surrogate families, their adopted sons, so many of whom went to their rest, suddenly and violently one night, forty-seven, forty-eight, or forty-nine years ago.

Taken over Pforzheim on the night of February 23/24, 1945, from a 156 Squadron aircraft, piloted by F/L Jackson. (Taff Jones)

Aircrew of 156 Squadron, May, 1944, R.A.F. Upwood.

(Taff Jones)

The placard in the photograph reads:

156 SQDN. P.F.F.
% C/c. BINGHAM-HALL
D.S.O. D.F.C.
AT R.A.F. STATION.
UPWOOD. MAY. 1944.

G/C. BINGHAM-HALL with 'Poppy'

G/C Bingham-Hall. D.S.O., D.F.C., with 'Poppy' and pilots of 156 Squadron. Taken at Upwood in May 1944.

(Taff Jones)

CHAPTER 6

NOT BERLIN AGAIN

*'Target bombed through cloud from 20,000 feet. Fires
seen to be burning and glowing through clouds. Very
heavy, intense and accurately predicted flak over
target, also much fighter activity.'*

Entry in log book of P/O Philip Wadsworth for a
Berlin raid.

The great assault on Berlin began on November 18th. Favourable weather
conditions existed, and it was decided to offer a diversionary raid (mostly
Halifaxes and Stirlings) to Ludwigshafen-on-Rhine. Another novel feature of
the planning was the reduction of the timing of the raid. 440 aircraft would
attack the 'Big City' over a period of sixteen minutes, and at a rate of over
twenty-seven per minute. This intentional rapid 'swamping' of the target would
then be an effective counter measure to the German Wild Boar night fighters.
    Twenty-one aircraft took off from Warboys. The weather was clear, and
W/C White, a flight commander, was the first to take off at 17.04, F/S Cromarty
the last at 17.30. Two aircraft had to return early, after jettisoning their bombs
in the North Sea. In one of the aircraft the rear gunner suffered from frostbite,
with the oxygen supply iced up. In the other a similar problem had developed
due to a failure in the heating system, so that the mid-upper gunner became
badly frostbitten.
    The crews had no idea that this was to be the start of what historians would
call the Battle of Berlin. Berlin had been previously attacked in two raids at the
end of August, and in early September, and it was obvious to all aircrew that
after the Ruhr and Hamburg, the Big City was next on the list. There had been
great plans to have ready for this operation the new and improved H2S Mark
III device, which would give a clearer target picture. In the event only one was
carried in an aircraft of another Pathfinder squadron. Immediately north of the
target, white drip flares showed the way, and provided an effective corridor;
thick cloud, however, made it an H2S attack, and the supporters and backers-
up bombed on the red T.I.s. Nevertheless the attack was very scattered. Because
of the cloud the defences could not really deploy their strength in the usual

64

sophisticated and co-ordinated way. Skymarker flares simply drifted down to be swallowed up by cloud, cloud so dense that the ground searchlights could not penetrate it. 'Moderate heavy flak and slight light flak with few searchlights, which were ineffective', the verdict of P/O Sloper, was one expressed in similar terms by many 156 crews. Of the three Lancasters shot down by flak over the target, one was from 156 Squadron and captained by W/C White.

John White, a gallant and distinguished flight commander of twenty-eight, had been Deputy Master Bomber on the Peenemunde raid. In two of Martin Middlebrook's books the significant contribution this officer made is heavily underlined. S/L Anset, another senior operational pilot, reported that three minutes before bombing he saw at 20.56 an aircraft fall in flames with red and yellow T.Is cascading from it. It is apparent that this must have been John White's aircraft, as, according to Middlebrook, the other two aircraft which fell over the target were from the main force. The Wing Commander's aircraft had five D.F.Cs flying in it, and two D.F.Ms, and all perished together.

One of the members of W/C John White's crew was Michael Stoneley. Michael Stoneley, the crew wireless operator, was from Belfast in Northern Ireland, and within two weeks of going missing, he had been awarded the D.F.M., and a commission. His friend Paddy McCrum (W/O J. McCrum D.F.M.) who had come to Pathfinders and 156 from 103 Squadron, was a wireless operator in another crew, that of F/O H. G. M. Taylor, D.F.C., C.G.M., who was subsequently killed when flying on the Met. Flight with 8 Group, 1409 Flight, from Oakington on December 5th, one of the three aircraft lost by this flight in its entire existence. Paddy McCrum was also a native of Belfast. This is something very typical of Bomber Command, and of Pathfinders, that these two friends from Belfast, both W/Op/AGs, should be flying in the same Pathfinder squadron, but in separate crews, with one taken and the other left. The children of both men attended the famous Methodist college, Belfast, after the war, where, in 1961, Michael Stoneley's daughter was Head Girl.

F/S Cromarty, who was showing promise as an operational pilot, was the first to land from this first Berlin raid of the 'Battle' at 11.36pm. It took until 01.39 hours in the morning for the eighteen survivors to land at Warboys. Nine aircraft were missing from the force that went, the lowest loss rate in the Battle, 2.0 per cent of aircraft dispatched to Berlin. Twenty-three aircraft from the mixed force that had proceeded to Ludwigshafen were also missing. It seems that the fighters had been successfully diverted from Berlin, and yet there had been this price to pay in Halifax and Stirling losses. Not a good or effective raid, this first Berlin one, it was thought. As always, on trips to Berlin, the great enemy on such a long flight of up to eight hours, apart from the flak and the fighters, was the weather. This winter offensive was to test the skill and endurance and courage of all crews, especially of the Pathfinders, whose timing and reliability in planting markers was depended upon by the whole force. On this raid the blind marking had not worked out. There were lessons to be learned for the future.

All that the tired crews sought on their return was the relief of clean sheets. Many, however, could not get the roaring of the engines out of their ears. For others the hot tea laced with rum at debriefing caused oblivion to descend almost immediately.

Four night later the Pathfinders sent 121 aircraft to Berlin, a record number out of a total of 764 aircraft sent out. Bad weather had intervened since the last raid, and had provided a much needed rest period for Bomber Command crews. The morning of November 22nd had an ideal weather forecast, good 'Berlin weather', clear conditions over home aerodromes, with fog or low cloud over the target. Unlike the previous Berlin raid, this was a maximum effort, 764 aircraft, with almost every operational squadron taking part. At Warboys twenty-one aircraft detailed for the raid took off. A new method of marking the target, whatever the cloud or weather conditions, was used for the first time on this raid. Target indicators and skymarkers were to be used throughout. Those using H2S Mark III equipment were called 'Special Blind Markers' with their own coloured T.Is. If they could be seen, the T.Is were bombed, as they were more accurate. If not, the skymarkers were the ones to go for. Equally H2S equipment was used throughout, but only acted upon when it could produce information of unimpeachable reliability. After the last raid on Berlin, a complaint had been received at Pathfinder H.Q. from 156 Squadron about the unreliability and continual technical difficulties of H2S sets. The Group Commander, Don Bennett, used this complaint as a peg on which to hang the firm instruction that in uncertain conditions H2S was a back up rather than the architect of victory in any single Pathfinder led raid. Old fashioned navigational skills were still what counted most.

On this operation the marking was concentrated, with Special Blind Markers, Blind Markers and Backers-Up providing few gaps in the process as it developed. The bombing began at 8.00pm and a large explosion was noticed by many Pathfinder crews, including those of 156, at 8.22pm. All 156 crews identified the target by both skymarkers and T:Is, even if they could not make a visual identification; three crews, used their H2S equipment, and in addition, checked their position by looking for the skymarkers or T.Is at the appropriate place.

P/O Rose saw an explosion just before the target area with red and yellow T.Is falling out of the centre of the explosion. This was obviously a Pathfinder aircraft hit by flak, and was logged by that crew for the intelligence report.

Two aircraft from the squadron were missing that night, those of S/L Anset and F/S Stephens. 'Tiny' Anset was a friend of Sam Hall. His virtuoso performances on the piano, his clear tenor voice singing arias from *La Bohème*, as well as cleverly executed comic songs, had been much in demand during stand downs and Mess parties, as we have heard in the previous chapter. He was, again, a senior operational pilot who had been awarded the D.F.C. only ten days before. One feature of this period of bomber operations was that curious sensation of watching your friends go into the night and disappear. It is unlikely that you would know well an entire crew. The Navigators' Trade Union stuck together, pilots tended to know pilots, engineers engineers, amd so on, with the youthfulness of the gunners providing a useful and utterly necessary measure of boisterousness. Friends on a Pathfinder squadron were friends for just a few months, and were usually parted by death. Their memory is just as poignant to-day, as I have learned in speaking to veterans at 156 reunions.

The pilot of the other missing aircraft, F/S Stephens, had been on the squadron only four months, which was the mean average for those who did not live to become veterans or even survivors. Even so, much had happened to this young pilot. On August 23rd that same year, when he had only been one month on the squadron, he nursed a crippled Lancaster from Berlin back to Warboys, and was awarded an instant D.F.M., together with two other N.C.Os in his crew. These two crews from the squadron were among twenty-six aircraft missing from this operation. A further six crashed in the appallingly bad weather which had characterised and would continue to characterise these winter operations to Berlin in late 1943 and early 1944. One aircraft of the twenty-one dispatched had returned early. Notwithstanding these casualties this second Berlin raid was reckoned a good raid, with bombing concentrated, and maintained on a night when the target was invisible and blanketed under ten tenths cloud, and the old enemies of frostbite within and icing outside the aircraft were as lethal as anything the Germans threw up. A return in the small hours, a sleep of utter fatigue for just a few hours, and squadron crews were summoned to attend the crew rooms shorrtly before noon. 'Ops' were on again that same night. There had been little respite for the tired aircrews. For the ground crews, having snatched a few hours of sleep in the flight huts waiting for their own particular aircraft to return, there was the prospect of another day working flat out, and a night of only fitfully snatched sleep.

Twenty aircraft were detailed and the target was again Berlin. All but one took off, and found, as before, the target totally obscured by cloud, but with a fitful glow beneath the cloud marking the fires of the previous night. The Pathfinder method of target marking was, again, the so-called 'Berlin method', explained in the description of the previous night's operation. Over the target the air was heavy with fighter flares, with the flak reducing in height to accommodate the passage through the sky of Wild Boar night fighters. From this operation P/O Rose, commissioned only two months ago, and awarded the D.F.C. six weeks before, failed to return with his crew. Those crews who did return found impenetrable fog at some of the stations, as well as on the final leg, and F/S Fordyce crashed at Bircham Newton just over the Norfolk coast. Three members of the crew were killed, while the remaining four were injured. The further detail that four of the nineteen aircraft which took off for Berlin on that night, November 23rd, had made an early return indicates the difficulty of mounting a Berlin operation two nights running. Indeed these four were among forty-six which had returned early that night. It was well nigh impossible to service under such pressure aircraft which could give night after night a perfect performance under such implacable weather conditions, flown as they often were to the limit of their endurance.

This was the heaviest Pathfinder loss, so far in the Berlin offensive, in proportion to the previous raids, and the losses on these raids of aircraft of other groups. Over all Pathfinder squadrons seven aircraft were shot down, and two others, in addition to that of F/S Fordyce, crashed in England. Neighbouring Wyton lost their C.O. that night, W/C Hilton, D.S.O., D.F.C. and Bar, after only three weeks in charge of 83 Squadron. The mortality of squadron C.Os is, as we shall see, one of the more arresting factors in the sad losses of this period.

The next Berlin raid for the squadron, on 26th November, was a fortunate one for 156, the only one in the series of Berlin raids of this period in which all aircraft dispatched returned safely. Twenty-one aircraft were involved, and just past Frankfurt the bomber stream split into two, with 157 Halifaxes and twenty-one Lancasters turning southwards towards Stuttgart, and 443 Lancasters making for Berlin. One novel feature of this raid was the release over the target, four minutes before the first Pathfinder aircraft came on the scene, of a great deal of 'Window'. This disrupted effectively those guns controlled by radar, and thus lowered the casualty rate for the Pathfinders. Although visibility was the clearest of any of the previous raids, and the crews could actually see the T.Is on the ground, the plan for the markers still relied upon H2S, in the classic 'Berlin method'. Both kinds of markers were dropped, whether the weather was clear or overcast, and the main force following bombed T.Is if they could see them, and skymarkers if they could not. A good, concentrated pattern emerged, after Blind Marker crews adjusted the bombing, skilfully directing it away from an earlier effort when Special Blind Markers had placed their flares several miles away from the aiming point. One factor on this raid worthy of mention is that inexperienced crews, now that the weather was clear, saw the Berlin defences at full stretch, and witnessed, possibly for the first time, their awesome power. Undoubtedly for some crews this was their first and last sight of the Berlin defences; twenty-eight Lancasters failed to return out of the 443 which attacked Berlin, and six Halifaxes were lost out of the 157 aircraft which had made so successful a diversion to Stuttgart. A further loss, which, once again, was becoming the sting in the tail of many operations was of twelve aircraft crashing in England on their return. South of Yorkshire thick fog enveloped all bases. It was an horrific experience: after the vigilance and strain and possible combat with German fighters of the previous few hours and the arm wrenching attempts on the part of the pilot to hurl the aircraft out of reach of the clinging grip of the searchlights, the last enemy became for some crews the treacherous fog of an English winter. For all aircrew crashing fatally at the home airfield, or so near it, was most feared. It was the most melancholy of deaths.

Once more there had been an increased loss rate. Warboys' good fortune was not shared by other stations, and out of the twenty-one aircraft sent out from the station on November 26th, three were abortive, early returns. From now until the end of the month bad weather prevented operations. This was, of course, both a welcome rest, and a chance for crews to sharpen their skills. If you looked in the sky during this period you would see aircraft engaged in a variety of activities, with pilots taking their Lancasters through endless corkscrew motions with British fighters on their tails. You would see aircraft returning from the bombing ranges at Whittlesey, after 'Y' training, or training with the special H2S equipment. The day after the last successful Berlin raid, there was a twenty-four hour stand down. Aircrew melted away in all directions. Liberty buses were arranged to Cambridge, or Peterborough, and the Golden Lion at St. Ives, or the Pike and Eel at Holywell did their usual roaring trade, as Warboys aircrew met friends and rivals from Wyton. The next raid would come soon enough, and aircrew, strange to say, had the capacity, such was the kind of war they fought, to erase from their minds the horror of the previous few days of intense operational experience.

On December 2nd the call went out for a maximum effort to Berlin. Fog caused most of the Yorkshire Halifaxes to be removed from the battle order later in the day. Nevertheless, 453 aircraft set out. Nineteen crews of 156 took off in the late afternoon from 5.11pm. onwards facing the customary hazards of cloud, icing on wings, and winds which were a navigator's nightmare, and bore no relation to those forecast by Met. at briefing. At 20.05 to 20.08 hours squadron crews saw the first T.Is and skymarkers cascading over the target. Bombing was done at 20.16 hours from 19,000 feet. The crew reports speak of a concern to correct or compensate for stray T.Is. S/L Manifold, for example, reports:

'At time of bombing there was a very good concentration of Reds and Greens in compact area, but a few of these fell in open country at least five miles from this concentration to the west. South of main concentration there was a big white fire which may have been incendiaries burning. Much smoke seen.'

Many aircraft that night were well off track due to the variable winds earlier mentioned. The night fighters had one of their field days in what was really good visibility. The total cost of the operation was that forty aircraft were missing, many of them the victims of night fighters. Lanes and corridors of fighter flares made this a hair-raising experience for crews. Twenty to twenty-five minutes was the time it took to run the gauntlet of the Berlin defences. Sadly, the bombing results on this occasion were not good. Crews, including some from 156, reported clusters of T.Is and incendiaries burning in open country. Post-war historians, and those who have conducted surveys of the allied bombing effort, estimated that three-quarters of the bombs delivered that night were scattered over open fields. Once again, the H2S Mark III equipment carried by Pathfinder aircraft of other squadrons had not turned out to be helpful.

Operational conditions had caused three out of the four aircraft carrying the equipment to turn back, and the fourth not to use its indicators lest others might be confused.

Three 156 crews failed to return, F/L Staniland, W/O Wicks, and F/S Redfern. The crew of F/L Staniland had been with the squadron exactly two months, W/O Wicks and crew had been with 156 a shorter time, while the crew of F/S Redfern had gone missing on their first trip with the squadron. There was one survivor from all these crews, F/S MacDonald from W/O Wicks' crew, who became a P.O.W. There were no 'easy' targets to give crews experience at this stage in the bomber offensive, and, like some Pathfinder crews, many main force crews did their first few trips to Berlin and equally ferocious targets.

The next night, December 3/4th, there was an extremely successful raid. The bomber stream feinted on Berlin, and, leaving the turn as late as possible, turned due south to Leipzig, while ten Mosquitoes (six from 139 Squadron and four from 627 Squadron) dropped 'Window' on the route to Berlin, and T.Is on the capital, drawing out all the Wild Boar fighters to Berlin. Over Leipzig only three combats with night fighters took place. Thirty per cent of Leipzig was destroyed. Because of the presence of ten-tenths cloud, skymarkers or *Wanganui* flares were needed. For the first time H2S Mark III aircraft did their job well, aided by the light winds which did not scatter the skymarkers. Among 156 crews, F/O Aubert reported that the glow could be seen from Frankfurt. Here, however, the German defences did exact a kind of revenge, and twelve aircraft were lost.

The Battle of Berlin had started well for Bomber Command. The most recent raid (December 2/3rd) was definitely a poor one, and the previous one (November 26/27th) was only average. The first three raids, however, were a definite success, although casualty figures were inexorably creeping up. For 156 Squadron the offensive had been costly, with eight crews missing in under three weeks since the Berlin offensive started on November 18th. It was to remain costly for 156 Squadron to the bitter end.

'Black Thursday' and a Costly Winter.

The next Berlin raid was not until December 16th. Since the last Berlin raid (December 2/3rd), and the successful Leipzig raid on the following night, there had been a series of raids by Mosquito aircraft on a number of targets, and a seemingly endless succession of training flights for 156. Four new crews were posted to the squadron and a number of crewless individuals to fulfil various aircrew duties. All the new crews had done a number of operations on other squadrons. There was no time in the Berlin offensive to train new crews from the conversion units and O.T.Us up to the required Pathfinder standards. Inevitably it happened that crews did join 156 fresh from one of the conversion units, but only those whose members achieved above average grades. The

Pathfinder Navigation Training Unit down the road at Upwood was always a useful provider of crews, and many if not most crews from another, main force squadron coming to 156 received a final 'lick and polish' at Upwood before joining the muddy front line station at Warboys.

On December 16th 483 Lancasters and fifteen Mosquitoes were dispatched to Berlin. The fear was, on planning this raid, that the weather would close in on the home bases. The other fear was the three quarter moon that would rise during the night. For these reasons there was an early take off time. F/L Aubert was the first to take off at 4.23pm., of the twenty-one aircraft from 156 which took off. His aircraft failed to return, the only one of those sent out from the squadron. Another unfortunate squadron casualty was that of F/S Watkins and all of his crew except the rear gunner. This pilot, recently arrived at Warboys, bombed the target at 9.01pm, and yet, on arriving home, crashed within a few miles of the aerodrome close to the Earith to Sutton road, two miles south west of Sutton, a location, even to-day, notoriously prone to bad weather. All the crew were killed, with the exception of the rear gunner, Sgt. Darlison, who was admitted to Ely R.A.F. Hospital. The fact that this aircraft had bombed the target in company with crews from the squadron was ascertained from the navigator's plotting charts, recovered from the wreckage of the aircraft. F/S Watkins was not the only one to crash that night. The fog that had been forming in eastern England accounted for the loss of thirty-four Lancasters. Some crashed with few or any survivors, crews collided over the home base, while some aircraft were abandoned, while crews baled out. Over the fens, Pathfinder country, fog was utterly impenetrable, and twelve Pathfinder Lancasters crashed. The Pathfinder squadron at Bourn lost seven aircraft, the majority of crew members being killed.

The tragedy of this 'Black Thursday' (as it was called in the annals of Bomber Command) blighted utterly what had, in fact, been a promising raid. There had been punctual and accurate marking by the Pathfinders, and concentrated bombing by the main force, and that in spite of the fact that crews of 156 reported dummy red and green T.Is. The majority of those twenty-five aircraft officially classified as 'missing' (which did not include crash victims) were shot down, it is thought, by flak. Certainly few enemy fighters were seen by the crews. The fog which caused such havoc to our returning bombers had effectively grounded most of the opposition.

The missing pilot from 156 squadron, F/L Aubert, D.F.M., was another experienced operational captain. Six members of this crew were decorated. Like many squadron pilots and aircrew members, including the author's father, F/L Aubert had joined the squadron from a main force squadron via 1662 Conversion Unit at Blyton. Several pilots my father flew with as an instructor on this conversion course ended their lives flying with 156. A pencilled asterisk against their names in my father's log book indicates the 'Burton symbol'. Such a symbol is placed against the name of F/O Aubert (as his rank was at that time) for a familiarisation flight in a Halifax V for August 3rd, 1943. Time and again in the literature of the bomber offensive, the severe losses of experienced crews in the Berlin offensive are underlined, crews and personnel which could not be replaced to the same level of experience and effectiveness. You could replace a lost crew with proficient, highly qualified youngsters (and it was possible to enter Pathfinders this way). The experience of a veteran crew, however, just could not be replaced. And the war the Pathfinders fought demanded experience, as well as courage. The night skies over Berlin from November 1943 to March 1944 were no place for the neophyte, whether he was from Pathfinders or main force. The fact that many crews made their debut at this time is an eloquent testimony to their courage, as to the need of the Group Commander for constant replacements. Very few of the neophyte crews would survive this period.

After this unhappy raid there was a gap of three days before a raid to Frankfurt was laid on, on December 20th, with a diversion to Mannheim. Twenty-one aircraft took off from Warboys, and two failed to return. F/L Sullivan, D.F.C., and F/O Watts and their crews. F/L Sullivan D.F.C. was leading a crew of decorated veterans, another irreplaceable loss. On this night combats between our aircraft and night fighters took place on both targets. You could say that the night fighters were not deceived by the spoof raid. Over Frankfurt P/O Bond, on successfully bombing the target, was attacked three times. Both gunners in the crew performed valiantly in driving off these attacks. The mid-upper gunner, P/O Moon, was wounded in his lung and right shoulder, and was admitted to hospital in Ely when the aircraft returned home. P/O Bond hurled his aircraft all over the night sky in a skilful evasion routine, and nursed the badly damaged Lancaster to Warboys, landing brilliantly, burst tyre and buckled wheel notwithstanding. The pilot and both gunners were decorated for this action. Both officers received D.F.Cs while the rear gunner, F/S Underwood, was awarded the D.F.M. Only P/O Moon survived to keep his 'appointment in London', and that was simply because of the lengthy hospital treatment and convalescence following this night's activities. The rest of the crew had only twelve more days to live.

Another 156 crew had an eventful night. This time it was the only crew from the squadron to contribute to the Mannheim diversion. A JU88 attacked the aircraft of F/L R. G. F. Stewart, after he had bombed the target, destroyed the rear gunner's turret, and made three further passes, during which the Lancaster was severely damaged. When the aircraft was hit and blazing, the JU88 suddenly broke off the attack, presumably because the pilot had run out of ammunition. Now began the crew's battle with the fire. Having successfully quenched the flames, they were attacked by an ME109, causing further fire in the aircraft which was effectively mastered yet again. Owing to the Lancaster's burst tyre F/L Stewart landed at Bungay, the U.S.A.A.F. base with the lengthy runway. For F/L Stewart a promotion to Squadron Leader followed, and, when he met his end twelve days later, on the same Berlin raid as P/O Bond (January 3rd 1944), there were five decorated members in his crew. Many of the men who were decorated for gallantry like that displayed on the night of December 20/21st did not live to receive their decorations at an investiture. Parents and widows made the journey to Buckingham Palace on behalf of those loved ones who had gone missing.

Three nights later F/L Stewart and his crew were on the battle order for Berlin. Night fighter activity necessitated some feints and changes of course. The Berlin raids in the past had commonly set off during the late afternoon, with aircraft returning at midnight. The weather forecast was now good, however, and the raid had to be set back by several hours, a frustrating experience for the crews, who must have thought the operation was going to be scrubbed. Eventually sixteen out of the nineteen aircraft detailed for operations did take off at around half past midnight. Only 390 aircraft were operating that night, a reflection of the losses sustained during the previous Berlin raid, and the Frankfurt operation. The losses were indeed light on this night, with fifteen aircraft missing and two more crashing in this country shortly after take-off. Crews of 156 spoke of some bombs and incendiaries falling short, others reported an attack spreading from west to east of the city, and talked of the ineffectiveness of 'spoof fighter flares'. The aircraft and crew of F/O Warfield, D.F.M., failed to return. 156 Squadron was making a steady loss of one, two and sometimes three aircraft per raid. This was the price for the extensive damage done to Berlin which the daylight photographs, obtained by reconnaissance aircraft two days before this raid, showed. The reconnaissance photographs gave a picture of devastation of more than 3,200 acres, of which over 2,500 acres belonged to the centre of the city. In the industrial areas many factories producing high-priority goods for the German war effort were damaged, some of them quite severely. So, although this last raid left a lot to be desired in terms of bombing results, the systematic destruction of Berlin was proceeding apace.

The Christmas period was marked by the usual stand down on December 25th, with parties and energetic celebrations. The stand down continued during the next day, while on the 27th and 28th training flights took place. You simply could not afford not to train when not operating. On December 29th it was Berlin again. Twenty-one aircraft took off from Warboys out of a total of 712 dispatched. Most 156 crews reported a good concentration of skymarkers 'spread out slightly in line east to west'. 'It should have been a good attack,' was the reaction of one flight commander, W/C Deane. For all these reactions, when the cloud had cleared it was evident that the bombing was more scattered than the enthusiastic verdicts of crews at debriefing could testify. There was a difficulty about knowing how you had done in an aircraft over Berlin in such weather conditions. You could bomb on skymarkers or T.Is, or bomb after a timed run, or by H2S. Often the photographs brought back did not reveal more than that you had obeyed instructions. That was all that could be asked of these gallant men. As F/L Stewart observed in his report after noting the fall of the red and green *Wanganui* flares:

'T.Is not seen owing to cloud. Two explosions – one at 2020 hours and another about 2022. Cloud obscured other observations.'

A 'double spoof' diversion by Mosquitoes, one to Magdeburg and the other to Leipzig, had left the German fighters guessing. When they finally arrived over Berlin, it was too late. Twenty aircraft were lost on this raid, none of them from Warboys, although there had been one early return. To find the weather clear over the home base was an unaccustomed luxury. In two days time this luck would change. On the first day of 1944, out of eighteen aircraft detailed for another Berlin raid four would not return. As in one of the previous raids there was uncertainty over the weather, and so take off time was put back to a time after midnight, so that the raid took place in the first few hours of January 2nd, with the first away, F/L Ralph, taking off at twenty minutes past midnight.

This was an all Lancaster raid, 421 of them, with a diversionary raid by Mosquitoes to Hamburg. On the way to the target eight aircraft in the marking force were shot down, and one was hit on its bomb run, and exploded. Pathfinders in general, and, as we have seen, Warboys in particular, lost heavily in this raid. Ten were lost out of an entire Pathfinder force of eighty-one. Of the four missing from 156 Squadron were the two crews who performed so valiantly in the Frankfurt/Mannheim raid the previous month, captained by P/O Bond, D.F.C., and (as he now was) S/L R. G. F. Stewart, D.F.C. The other two missing crews were captained by S/L R. F. Fawcett. D.F.C. and by F/O T. Docherty. There were no survivors from these four crews. The crews piloted by S/Ls Stewart and Fawcett were among the most experienced in the entire Pathfinder force, let alone the squadron, while the crew of P/O Bond had had a meteoric and brilliant career on 156. S/L Fawcett's son was born posthumously, and I have met him and his mother at squadron reunions.

Those crews who survived this new year Berlin operation flew into Warboys between 7.00am and 7.30am. As the snow was falling, they considered it unlikely they would be operating that night. And yet they were awoken in mid-afternoon with the news that 'ops' were on again. It was to be another midnight take off, and, when the crews strode into the briefing room, and saw on the wall map the long ribbon going straight in to Berlin and straight out, with no diversions or dog legs, there was dismay. Fatigue was the enemy in a war in which alertness could mean the difference between life and death. All told, 383 aircraft were sent out. As in the previous raid eighteen Warboys aircraft were detailed for this operation. Four, however, could not be made serviceable in the time available, considering their state after the previous night's operation, and one returned early. After a midnight take off the bombers met with thick cloud, and flying conditions remained atrocious nearly up to the target itself. At 2.42am P/O Hopton saw the first red T.Is dropped over the target with a skymarker above it. Other crews noticed large gaps in the skymarkers and T.Is. By contrast, as in the previous night's raid, other crews looked at the skymarkers and thought how they seemed to form 'a good concentration in line above the target'. And again as in the previous night's operation, these breaks in the marking, these inadequacies are to be explained in terms of the mauling the Pathfinders received. Twenty-six aircraft were missing from the raid, nine of them Pathfinder crews, and five of them from 156 Squadron, P/O Borland, D.F.C., Sgt. Barnes, F/L Ralph, D.F.M., F/O Cairns and P/O Cromarty and crews. Four of Sgt. Barnes' crew survived. Thirty-two lives of 156 aircrew were lost in this one operation, twenty-eight the night before.

That same day, January 2nd, S/L Brooks was posted to Warboys from the Upwood N.T.U. He would replace one of the missing flight commanders. The aircraft of P/O Cromarty could not be found and his name and the names of his crew appear on the Runnymede memorial for those who have no known grave. Amazingly, their remains were found buried under earth and rubble in East Berlin in 1976 during some building work. They are now all interred in the Berlin War Cemetery with countless other bomber aircrew shot down over the 'Big City'. In addition five new replacement crews arrived at Warboys, three from 626 Squadron, and two in a sideways move from 7 Squadron, the Pathfinder Squadron at Oakington. Other breaches had to be repaired. The new C.O. of 83 Squadron, W/C Abercromby, had failed to return from the first Berlin operation of the year. One of 156 Squadron's flight commanders, W/C Dixie Deane, D.F.C. (who had led his crew on the raid to Berlin the night before) was posted on January 3rd to command 83 Squadron, and within the next five days four more replacement crews were posted to Warboys, and four individual officers. On January 5th, the squadron sent eighteen aircraft to Stettin, and, happily for the squadron's morale, seventeen returned safely and successfully, and one made an early return.

On January 14th twenty-one aircraft were detailed for an operation to Brunswick. These were new aircraft, some new crews, and a target that was not Berlin. So hopes were high. A late afternoon take off between 4.45pm and 5.00pm., and the bombers were over the target at 7.08pm. There is a tentativeness about the reports of the crews, reflecting perhaps the lack of bombing concentration on the previous two Berlin raids. And so we read in F/L Day's report:

'Results difficult to assess, but for a Wanganui attack they may not have been too bad.'

When the bombers returned to Warboys between 9.45pm and 10.45pm., five were missing. All of the five missing crews were veterans. W/C Mansfield, D.F.C., another flight commander, and his decorated crew had been with the squadron since June. As a Squadron Leader he was posted to 156 from 97 Squadron at Bourn on June 17th, 1943, together with the man who flew as his navigator, F/O Alexander, D.F.M. The night he died he was a Wing Commander with the D.F.C., and his navigator F/L Alexander, D.F.M. was gazetted Squadron Leader two days after going missing, and the D.F.C. was added to his

D.F.M. There were four D.F.Cs and three D.F.Ms in his crew. To trespass on my other profession, 'there were giants then in the land'. There is a passage in Don Bennett's book *Pathfinder* in which at about this time, in the winter of early 1944, he laments the loss of flight commanders, squadron commanders and experienced crews, and wonders whether the backbone of the Pathfinder force had not been broken. Out of these five missing Warboys crews, five men survived, to become P.O.W.s (F/O Illingworth and four of his crew) while thirty died. The total loss on the Brunswick raid, thirty-eight Lancasters out of the 498 aircraft dispatched was the most severe loss sustained by Bomber Command for weeks.

Warboys and 156 wondered how long casualties like this could continue: fourteen crews missing from the last four raids. Faces in the Mess were unfamiliar and it was sad to come back off leave to be told that the friend with whom you were at O.T.U. or the last conversion unit, or who was even a member of your regular crew was now missing. Small wonder that many crews wrote themselves off and decided to live from day to day. Replacement crews flooded in, keen to have a go. It was generally known that Pathfinders were having a bad time in this later stage of the Berlin battle. After all, eleven in total were missing from the Brunswick raid. But Warboys had earned her reputation as the Pathfinder chop squadron. The bad weather of the next five days was the time to rest, recuperate and prepare for the next operation. Meanwhile it was necessary to find new aircraft for the replacement crews to fly.

On January 20th operations were on, and the target was Berlin. Among the new crews whose first flight this was on 156 was a crew posted from 626 Squadron at Wickenby after four 'ops'. It was a fine day for take off at 4.44pm when Sgt. Jack Cuthill took off for Berlin. The rear gunner in this crew, Ron Smith, has vividly portrayed his experiences on 156 in a book, published by Goodall in 1987, entitled *Rear Gunner Pathfinders*. Ron Smith was a Yorkshireman as was the mid-upper gunner, Doug Aspinall. Jack Cuthill was a Canadian from British Columbia, Geoff Thornycroft, the navigator, was from Manchester, the bomb aimer, and second navigator, Bob Trotter, was from Durban, the wireless operator Ross Tobin was an Australian, while the flight engineer, Ron Breeze, was from South Wales. That was a typical mix in Bomber Command, and especially in Pathfinders, which had more than their share of men from the Dominions.

The raid caused extensive damage in Berlin, at a cost of thirty-five aircraft lost out of the 769 dispatched. Sgt. Cuthill's take off time, 4.56pm, was half an hour later than most of the rest of the squadron, as the emergency air cylinder was found to be empty, and needed to be topped up. The new crew caught up with the rest of the Pathfinders, and weaved all the way to Berlin. The bomb aimer and second navigator, Bob Trotter, was operating the H2S set, and Ron Breeze, the flight engineer, bombed the first T.Is seen going down. The crew were in the role of Supporters. In spite of medium flak over the target no ground detail could be observed, an experience shared by all crews.

The next day, January 21st, saw another operation, this time not to Berlin, but to Magdeburg, sixty miles west of Berlin. That was a late take off for crews of 156, round about 8.00pm., after chequered fortunes in preparing aircraft for the raid. Only fourteen out of the twenty-one detailed for operations set off, and two made early returns. Fighters were active over the target. The mid-upper gunner in Sgt. Cuthill's crew saw an ME110 with two rockets attached to it. The mid-upper gave him a burst, as well as the rear gunner, and the W/Op in the astrodome saw the tracer of the mid-upper gunner going home on the ME110. Diving away out of view, the enemy aircraft was seen no more. One aircraft was missing from Warboys, that of F/O Kilvington, D.F.C. and crew. The rear gunner in this aircraft, F/L Thomson, was responsible, so it has been concluded, for shooting down the ace of German night fighter pilots, Major Heinrich Prinz zu Sayn-Wittgenstein, who had a tally of eighty-three victories in the skies over Europe and in Russia. Happily all members of the crew survived, and became P.O.Ws in Stalag Luft 3. The bomb aimer, F/L Muggeridge, D.F.C. was a former member of 103 Squadron at Elsham Wolds, and was one of the many New Zealanders on 156. The entire crew had been on the squadron since September 1943, the classic average period of stay on the squadron for these many passing guests.

The Magdeburg raid had been a disaster. Winds were variable and some of the main force had arrived over the target before the Pathfinders, and twenty-seven had bombed without even waiting for T.Is. Thus, when the leaders of the Pathfinders arrived, there were no means of identifying the briefed aiming point. Decoy reds backed with greens drew off the bombing in most cases. Fifty-five bombers were missing from the raid, nine of them Pathfinders. The Pathfinder Squadron at Graveley lost three crews.

The day after the Magdeburg raid was the day when G/C Collings relinquished his command of the squadron. From June 8th 1943 he had commanded the squadron, while being Station Commander as well. He remained as Station Commander, but handed over the squadron to W/C E. C. Eaton, D.F.C., a younger man who had been posted to the squadron several days earlier from the conversion unit at Blyton, 1662, he commanded. W/C Eric Eaton, or 'Ginger' Eaton as he was popularly known, had previously commanded a front line operational squadron, 101, at Bourn in Cambridgeshire (now a Pathfinder station) and Holme-on-Spalding-Moor in Yorkshire from June 1942 to the end of January 1943.

So the squadron was girding itself for the new challenge. The losses were to be endured in the hope of better times. Meanwhile there were new crews, new aircraft, a new C.O., in combination with the maturity of experience of G/C Collings who stayed on as 'Station Master' (R.A.F. slang for Station Commander). To endure as C.O. the losses during the battles of the Ruhr earlier in 1943, and of Hamburg and in the winter of 1943 and early 1944 the crippling losses of the Berlin raids, to be in intimate touch with all the details of a front line squadron's life, while at the same time, as Station Commander, managing the thousand and one details of personnel establishment on a wartime aerodrome was something to tax the endurance of most men. During his period as C.O. from June 1943 G/C Collings had seen ninety-five crews come to Warboys. Only seventeen of these crews had survived.

After Magdeburg a rest for three nights. An 'op' was then planned for January 25th, and then cancelled. On Thursday January 27th 515 Lancasters and fifteen Mosquitoes set out for Berlin. Sixteen Lancasters took off from Warboys, and, with one early return, all of them returned to base. For a cost of thirty-five Lancasters the results of the bombing were only average. Among 156 crews F/L Mackay's aircraft was attacked by a fighter on coming up to the bomb run. Both gunners, F/S Stein and F/O Harris, were wounded, but the aircraft's captain pressed on. Having successfully bombed the target, he nursed home an aircraft which was badly crippled, with two wounded gunners on board. This was good 'press-on' stuff, and very much in the Pathfinder tradition. The very next night all but F/L Mackay's aircraft (fifteen aircraft) were out again to Berlin, a maximum effort this time totalling 677 aircraft. Again, all returned.

This was an unusual element for 156 crews: two successive trips to Berlin with no casualties! One night of rest, and the next trip to Berlin on January 30th broke the chain of good fortune. Out of sixteen Lancasters who took off there were two early returns and two missing. These two aircraft were shot down by fighters. One aircraft (JB302) was shot down over Berlin. The captain, W/O P. Batman, was able to bale out with two of his crew, to become P.O.Ws. The other Lancaster, captained by W/O Rule, was set on fire by a night fighter to the north of Hannover, and exploded. The wireless operator, Sgt. Coyne, was flung clear by the explosion and drifted through the night to fall on to Dutch soil. The navigator, Sgt. Cottom, so Sgt. Coyne discovered, had also made a miraculous escape. Both men eventually became P.O.Ws although Sgt. Coyne had numerous adventures, being passed along the line by the Dutch underground until he fell into the hands of the Gestapo in Antwerp seven months after baling out.

Thirty-three of our bombers were missing from this raid. Of eight Pathfinder aircraft lost that night three were from 405 Squadron at Gransden Lodge. Severe damage had been inflicted on the 'Big City' on this and on the previous raid. When the Pathfinder blind markers could get through, and, despite casualties they did get through on these raids and bomb the target successfully, the raid usually resulted in a successful bombing concentration.

A New C.O. - a new start.

With the coming of February, there was a prolonged stand down from operations. New crews were posted to 156, among them one captained by a Norwegian, 2nd Lt. F. Johnsen, with a Norwegian rear-gunner, Sgt. Karsman in the crew. On the last day of January there had been thirty-two mentions in dispatches for the arduous and prolonged work put in by ground personnel, and during this rest period several aircrew officers were awarded D.F.Cs and Bars to D.F.Cs. There were non-operational flights most days. Cross country flights to test out the H2S, known as 'Y' training, were sent out, and the usual, perpetual fighter affiliation flights, with many visits to the bombing ranges at Whittlesey.

On February 10th the King and Queen came to Warboys, visiting also Graveley and Gransden Lodge. It was a bitterly cold February morning. Photographs of the period show faces straining into the wind. Crews, aircrew and ground crews, are standing to attention, while the King and Queen pass along the ranks, escorted by A/V/M Bennett, G/C Collings and W/C Eaton. Some of those photographs taken at Warboys on that day have become classics, permanent records of their Majesties meeting the Pathfinders, in whose nightly doings they took, it is accredited, a deep interest. A photograph in my possession shows my father standing before the Queen and smiling. Ron Breeze recalls that he and his crew were asked questions about the operations they had done, and that he was favoured with a nice smile from the Queen. After the parade the royal couple had lunch in the Officers' Mess, before leaving for Graveley and Gransden Lodge. In a letter to my mother my father added:

'P.S. The King and Queen came to see me to-day.'

My father was now on the squadron. He was posted to 156 on January 24th, after his period as an instructor at 1662 conversion unit at Blyton. He did not come already crewed up. His last crew had been those he flew with at Elsham Wolds in Lincolnshire when he was on 103 Squadron. When W/C Eaton moved from commanding 1662 conversion unit at Blyton to take command of 156 Squadron, he quite literally came 'bringing his sheaves with him', in the shape of a number of experienced, tour expired aircrew. So P/O Philip Wadsworth joined the squadron, two days after G/C Collings relinquished command, and took part in a fighter affiliation flight on his first full day at Warboys, with G/C Collings (now Station Commander, rather than Squadron C.O.), as pilot.

One task a flight engineer in Pathfinders had to learn was to be ready to act as bomb aimer on certain raids, while the bomb aimer member of the crew worked the H2S set, and so virtually become a second navigator. There were a number of flights like this for the new Pathfinder flight engineer. The 'crewing up' process was a gradual process for the reserve aircrew the Wingco had brought over from Blyton. P/O Wadsworth was simply allocated an aircraft, Lancaster ND409, G for George, in 'B' flight, under the watchful eye of an experienced flight commander, S/L 'Dickie' Walbourn, in a crew which was eventually found (though changes went on being made). All the initial training flights were made with a variety of pilots, beginning with the Station Commander.

On February 13th, a Sunday, the long stand down from operations was over. It was to be Berlin. As the cloud ceiling lowered, with the crews already in their aircraft, bombed up and ready, the 'op' was scrubbed. This was the very worst, and the most frustrating thing to happen to operational aircrew, for an operation to be scrubbed, when everyone was at such a pitch of readiness. In these circumstances you had done the 'op' already in your mind. The more superstitious took it phlegmatically almost, with the feeling that an 'op' which was scrubbed might be the one you were to go missing on. 'Never curse a scrubbed op.' Finally on February 15th there came an operation.

Twenty-one Lancasters took off from Warboys shortly after 5.00pm, six of them as part of the diversionary force of twenty-four aircraft to attack Frankfurt-on-Oder while the rest were Berlin bound. They were to use H2S on this attack, in order to deceive the enemy into regarding this as a major attack, and draw the German fighters away from the Berlin area. The force attacking Berlin was a maximum effort, 891 aircraft. Let no one imagine this was an all-Lancaster force. There were 314 Halifaxes taking part, and sixteen Mosquitoes. The 'spoof' attack on Frankfurt-on-Oder drew no night fighters, while the Berlin bound force was harried from the east coast of Denmark all the way to the target, where they were handed over to the flak. They then took up the cudgels and pursued the returning bomber stream, when the aircraft emerged from the flak over the target. This was a classic German 'Tame Boar' operation, and forty-three bombers were missing.

On this raid the 'maximum effort' element was reflected in the 121 Pathfinder aircraft flying that night. The Frankfurt-on-Oder force returned without any loss. 'A rather uneventful trip' is the remark in my father's log book. He had flown with W/C Eaton among the six aircraft from 156 that went to Frankfurt-on-Oder. Both forces, over Berlin and over the diversionary target, had to bomb through ten tenths cloud, using skymarkers or *Wanganui* flares dropped by the Pathfinders. On this night one of the squadron's rear gunners, Sgt. G.C.C. Smith, was awarded the C.G.M. He was the rear gunner in F/S Ken Doyle's crew among the aircraft from 156 who went to Berlin. Two German fighters, an ME110 and an FW190, made a co-ordinated attack on F/S Doyle's, Lancaster before they arrived at the target. The two gunners, Sgt. A. C. Clarke, the mid-upper, and Sgt. Smith drove off the two fighters with their split-second instructions to the pilot and their use of their own guns. Indeed one of the enemy aircraft, the ME110, blew up as a result of their return fire. Both gunners, however, were wounded, the rear gunner so severely that his right leg had to be later amputated. The mid-upper gunner's left leg was broken, and the aircraft had to be brought in after the jettisoning of its bombs, in a badly damaged state, and on three engines, to an emergency landing at Warboys.

The squadron lost a veteran pilot and crew on this raid. F/L Stimpson, D.F.C. had been with 156 since the days of the Hamburg raids in July. He had come as a flight sergeant with his crew from 1662 conversion unit in July 1943, and went down on this raid as a flight-lieutenant with a D.F.C. Two other members of this crew had been awarded the D.F.C., and one the D.F.M. A few days earlier my father had been briefed to fly as F/L Stimpson's flight engineer in the 'op' to Berlin that was scrubbed on February 13th, when all Warboys crews were waiting in their aircraft on the runways and perimeter tracks to take off. It had been an unhappy night for the nearby Pathfinder squadron at Oakington. They had lost four aircraft, with some of the most experienced crews, including a wing commander and two squadron leaders.

Several days of bad weather, with fog anticipated on the airfields of eastern England meant a cancellation of raids after initial orders had been sent out to expect operations that night. On February 16th, 17th and 18th aircraft were detailed for operations to Berlin, night flying tests were carried out, and the operations were scrubbed. On the 19th, however, 'ops' were on. This time the target was not Berlin, but Leipzig, a high priority target with factories devoted to aircraft production. Indeed on this target, Leipzig, and on the next two, Schweinfurt and Augsburg the combined bomber offensive was really coming into its own, as they would be attacked both by R.A.F. Bomber Command, as well as by the U.S.A.A.F., with a few hours only between night and day attacks.

The Leipzig attack was a maximum effort. 832 bombers took off into scurrying snow. Twenty-one aircraft set out from Warboys, and marked the target in classic 'Berlin fashion' with *Wanganui* flares and T.Is. During the attack there was a gap of approximately four minutes, so crews observed, during which no markers were seen going down. This may have resulted from the confusion over the target caused by early arrivals, colliding bombers, and those who were dog legging, or simply hanging about in order to arrive over the target at their directed time. The cause of all this was the fact that the winds forecast at briefing, which allowed for a steady and severe wind coming straight at the aircraft, turned out to be a light, northerly wind. F/L Harry Wright, an Australian navigator on the squadron, briefed his pilot on the flight out to do deliberate dog legs or time wasting manoeuvres for some thirty-one minutes. Harry Wright had been one of Don Charlwood's friends on 103 Squadron, and had flown in the crew of S/L Cook, until he was sick and missed the raid on which the rest of the crew went missing. He was an experienced navigator, and so detected early on the flight the strength of the winds, and how much they differed from the information given at briefing.

On the whole Pathfinder crews were not misled by the problem of the wind. Ron Breeze, flight engineer in F/S Cuthill's crew, reports that his aircraft did 'quite a few dog legs to lose time', and that he acted as bomb aimer, on an H2S attack, bombing the centre of three red markers going down. He adds that 'the trip was the quietest yet made, no flak or searchlights'. The same could not be said of other aircraft in 156, or in the Command at large. Two crews, were found to be missing when the aircraft returned to Warboys, that of S/L Saunders, an experienced crew with four D.F.C.'s and a D.F.M. (who had only been posted from Oakington and 7 Squadron to make up for some of the terrible losses of that month on January 5th) and of W/O Stannery (who had moved to Warboys on January 19th from 166, a main force squadron based at Kirmington).

The next day, February 20th, saw an operation to Stuttgart, another long flight, like Leipzig had been, with a take off after midnight, a long slog through thick cloud, with the danger of icing, and an H2S attack, with *Wanganui* flares. The Leipzig raid had been of seven hours duration, while Stuttgart was six and a half hours plus. Small wonder that, as the Stuttgart raid developed, crew members, especially the gunners, who needed a particular kind of vigilance, sucked their benzedrine tablets. On the Stuttgart raid it was too foggy for night fighters to make effective attacks, although they were about. The German defence reverted to the classic flak barrage. Crews from 156, and Pathfinder crews in general brought back their T.Is, and bombed the skymarkers, since ten tenths cloud blanketed the target.

It had not been a good night for 156. Of the eighteen aircraft detailed for this operation, four did not take off, and there were three early returns. In the one aircraft which failed to return, piloted by F/L D. K. Mackay, D.F.C., the Squadron Gunnery Leader, S/L Muir, D.F.C., flew as rear gunner. This was another heavily decorated crew, with a section leader the squadron could ill afford to lose. F/L Mackay had earned his D.F.C. on a trip to Berlin on January 27th by bringing back to Warboys an aircraft badly damaged by an enemy aircraft and two wounded gunners. As we have seen, section leaders, like the gunnery leader travelling with F/L Mackay, were to prove particularly vulnerable in the casualties that occurred over the next few months. For the force as a whole that set out for Stuttgart that night, however, it had been a successful raid. A Munich diversion by twenty-four Mosquitoes had drawn off the German fighters, without loss to themselves; and only nine aircraft failed to return, while five more crashed in England on their return.

In the break of three nights which followed, three new crews were posted to Warboys. And then, on February 24th, came a new and different target, Schweinfurt, a name infamous in the annals of the U.S.A.A.F., who had sustained grievous casualties bombing the town that afternoon, and were to suffer other casualties on costly raids over this target.

The attack by Bomber Command on Schweinfurt in the evening was to be a two-pronged attack. The first one was to consist of 392 aircraft, and the second, taking off two hours later, was made up of 342 aircraft. The aircraft of F/S Cuthill was in the second wave, with a take off at 8.45pm., and an initial course which took the aircraft near London and into a Luftwaffe raid on the city. So a number of 156 Lancasters had to brave 'friendly' flak before leaving the English coast. Over the target which could be seen from 120 miles away, as Ron Breeze noted, the sky was 'deadly, coned by searchlights, and filled with flak'. Both bombing forces, in both waves of the attack, displayed a tendency to undershoot, Pathfinder backers-up, as well as main force crews. Thirty-nine aircraft were lost from the combined force of 734. Warboys lost three aircraft that night, W/C E. F. Porter, P/O S. W. G. Neighbour, and F/L J. A. Day, D.F.C.,with their crews. W/C Porter had joined the squadron from nearby Wyton in late November, P/O Neighbour and crew had come from 166 Squadron in December, while F/L Day and his crew had moved to the squadron in September from 103 Squadron at Elsham Wolds. Both F/L Day and three of his crew survived to become P.O.Ws. For the others their short stay on the squadron, the longest being only of three months duration, had taken them through the worst time in the squadron's history. One new face in the Mess and around the flight offices was that of W/C. W. G. Scott who was posted to the squadron the day of the Schweinfurt raid. All too often at this period in the history of Pathfinders and of the Command at large senior replacements were just not available. Where they did exist, they usually moved sideways from other Pathfinder Squadrons. There had been, for example, a lot of traffic between 7 Squadron at Oakington and 156, and between 97 Squadron at Bourn and our squadron at Warboys.

On the next day the pressure was maintained, and the target was Augsburg. Again, as in the case of previous targets visited recently, the U.S.A.A.F. had been there first, and had bombed in the afternoon. Also, just as in the case of Schweinfurt, so at Augsburg there were two phases of attack by the R.A.F. Eighteen Warboys Lancasters went out in the second wave of the attack, leaving at about 9.30pm. The route took them along the border of Switzerland where an aircraft was observed coned by thirty to forty searchlights, and having flak pumped into it. The Warboys aircraft also saw a Pathfinder aircraft burning fiercely just before they came to the target, with green T.Is cascading from it when it crashed far below them. On their bombing run the aircraft of Sgt. Cuthill nearly collided with a JU88. Ron Breeze reported that 'it was about ten feet above us, and I could see the numbers painted on it'. Near the French coast, on the return journey, an enemy fighter made two passes at the aircraft, but the pilot successfully evaded the fighter by the most violent corkscrewing. Out of the 594 aircraft which had set out that night twenty-one were lost, one from 156, that of F/S Millen and crew. They had been with the squadron an even shorter time than the crews lost over Schweinfurt. Only one member survived in F/S Millen's crew, the navigator, F/S Yeomans.

It had now become known throughout the squadron that a move was imminent, and that 156 would soon transfer from Warboys to Upwood. Current roles would then be reversed, with Warboys having the Pathfinder N.T.U. (the Navigation Training Unit) and Upwood being the squadron's new operational home. So it was that on February 27th an advance party of one officer and sixteen men proceeded to R.A.F. Upwood. It would be a few more days before the aircraft of the squadron made Upwood their home. Meanwhile it was 'ops' as usual.

A new station.

The last operation from Warboys took place on March 1st, with a late take off to Stuttgart, ten minutes before midnight. Eighteen aircraft from Warboys climbed up into the midnight snow and there was thick cloud present as the 557 aircraft made their way to the target. Ten tenths cloud over the target meant that both T.Is and *Wanganui* flares were overwhelmed, and that reflections were only fitful, and hard to see. Ron Breeze, acting as bomb aimer in F/S Cuthill's crew writes of the typical problems facing a Pathfinder crew under conditions like these

'We did not drop our T.Is or skymarkers because our special equipment was u/s. I was bombing, and followed two skymarkers around the target, but they went out before I could get them into my bombsights. So I dropped them on E.T.A.'

As the bombers returned to Warboys it was early morning (6.30am to 7.15am). They had seen the dawn rise, while over the Channel, a beautiful sight for any returning bomber crew. The squadron was missing one aircraft, that night, the Lancaster of F/S Baker and crew. They had been posted from 460 Squadron on January 14th, and had been at Warboys only six weeks.

After the raid to Frankfurt-on-Oder my father had gone on leave, returning to the squadron on March 3rd just as the move to Upwood was imminent. Once back on the squadron he met his pilot F/O Gillmore, and the crew with whom he was to fly on operations for the rest of his time on 156 was now complete. There were other operations on which the C.O. captained the aircraft but from now on P/O Wadsworth became a member of F/O Gillmore's crew. After a day spent in 'Y' training and a lengthy cross country flight, the entire squadron moved to Upwood. The Lancasters had all moved to the new base, a few miles away, by 11.00am., and convoys of trucks with ground personnel and equipment thundered along north of Warboys in the direction of Ramsey. The word had come through that 'ops' were on that night. Fortunately, they were scrubbed, and the move was completed in its entirety by 6.00pm that evening. W/C/Eaton remained C.O. of 156, of course, while the Station Commander was G/C J.L. Airey, D.F. C., a man the aircrews and all Upwood personnel were to come to hold in much affection.

The next day, March 6th, 'ops' were on, night flying tests were completed in the morning, and the aircraft were standing on the runways waiting for the green, when the 'op' was cancelled. My father was sitting in the flight engineer's seat alongside F/L Slade in Lancaster ND543 when the scrub was signalled. F/L Slade was to have a distinguished career on·156. He completed three operational tours, earned the D.S.O. and D.F.C., and acted as Master Bomber on a number of raids before returning to his native Australia.

The next 'op', on March 8th, was again cancelled, after night flying tests done in the afternoon. This was the worst time for aircrew. After a number of scrubs, they had to operate.

On March 15th the opportunity came: it was Stuttgart again, the third attack on this city in the last few weeks. A quiet take off just as dusk was falling, and a journey with vigorous head winds, much stronger than those forecast by Met. at briefing, making the aircraft seven minutes late (both Pathfinders and main force). This was inevitably a scattered raid, with the crews doing the marking arriving late and at intervals, so that there was no continuous backing up on the markers. It is illuminating to read the sober reporting of Ron Breeze upon a raid which, from the description of events, could well have been the last for F/S Cuthill and his crew.

'The skymarkers were going down in all directions. It was very scattered. There were no searchlights over the target, but flak was pretty thick, bursting about 17,000 feet. As we left the target we were nearly rammed by two Lancasters and a Halifax. They passed about ten feet above the rear turret. I also saw a FW190 going after a Halifax. He didn't see us. Just after leaving the target area we were dived on by a twin-engined aircraft but took evasive action and lost him. We saw a few more aircraft burning on the way back, shot down by fighters. It was pretty quiet on the return. Except for a bit of flak over towns, we saw nothing.'

Forty aircraft were missing out of the 850 which had set out. None were missing from Upwood, All returned. The *Operations Record Book* has a note after this raid, stating:

'The previous occasion on which twenty-four aircraft proceeded, and all returned was on July 24th 1943.'

This was something to boost the confidence of squadron crews, at the time when the Berlin offensive was drawing to a close.

Meanwhile new crews and individual aircrew were joining the squadron all the time. Just before the move to Upwood S/L Thomas, D.S.O., D.F.M.who had a distinguished record as a navigator on 156, and had served as Squadron Navigation Leader, was posted to the H.Q. of 3 Group. His successor was S/L J. F. Hacking. D.F.C. and Bar. In the early days at Upwood F/S Cleland and crew arrived from 12 Squadron at Wickenby. At Upwood he rose to become a senior operational captain, as did F/L R. F. Griffin, Frank Griffin, who arrived with his crew at Upwood from 103 Squadron on the very day of the successful Stuttgart 'op'. Frank Griffin, a Devonian, was to go into commercial flying after the war, like quite a number of 156 survivors. He was piloting the Lancastrian that landed in Bermuda ahead of the ill-fated *Star Tiger* of British South American Airways in January 1946, which disappeared into the Atlantic Ocean.

A few days after F/L Griffin came to the squadron, F/L T. E. Ison and his crew came to Upwood. 'Tiny' Ison was to become one of the most experienced pilots on the squadron, and ultimately to become the squadron C.O.

Three nights after the Stuttgart 'op' there was a switch to Frankfurt. F/S Cuthill's crew were again destined for an exciting night. It was still light at 7.30pm. when the Upwood crew were taking off. Ron Breeze writes:

'Just as we got to the target we were attacked by a JU88 accompanied by a ME109. The rear gunner fired a three second burst at him, and he broke away. We were diving and taking evasive action. It came in again to attack us, but the rear gunner again fired at him with a five to six second burst. He broke away again as strikes were observed on him. The ME109 made off. I had to bomb with

the bomb sight then because our "Y" run was spoiled. I bombed the centre of green T.Is seen. Fires were burning furiously on the ground, but no details could be seen. We were flying through the shell bursts and just in front of us on top of the target I saw a Lancaster blow up. A terrifying sight.'

Lancaster ND409 G for George had a much quieter trip than this. P/O Wadsworth notes in his log:

'Bombed from 18,000 feet, through eight tenths cloud and considerable haze. Attack well concentrated. Uneventful trip, in spite of heavy flak over target area.'

On return to Upwood, once again no aircraft were lost from 156 Squadron although twenty-two were lost from the whole Command. As on the previous trip, twenty-four had set out, and all had successfully returned. There was a flicker of hope around the Messes and flight offices. Perhaps it might be possible to survive. Had the tide turned? The quite obvious turning away from Berlin and its savage casualties was giving the crews a welcome and vital breathing space. The feeling was compounded by another casualty free raid on Frankfurt three days after the last one, March 22nd.

The pattern of this second Frankfurt raid clearly resembled the first. An early take off from Upwood of twenty-one aircraft gave aircrew the novel experience of seeing other Lancasters flying alongside them, as it gradually grew darker over the North Sea. Over the target it was another well concentrated attack through five tenths cloud, and crews reported heavy flak, and huge searchlight concentrations. Thirty-three aircraft were lost on this raid, and much damage had been done to this important city. Three casualty-free raids were a novelty for the 'chop squadron'. As we shall see, 156 needed this respite badly. Other squadrons were less fortunate. No. 7 Squadron at Oakington lost their C.O. on this second Frankfurt raid, G/C K. Rampling, D.S.O., D.F.C., the first of three C.Os in succession to be lost on operations.

The day after the raid, S/L Geoghegan, another experienced navigator was posted away from the squadron. He was posted only a few miles away, to the Pathfinder N.T.U., now at Warboys, who were badly in need of navigators of proven operational skill and experience. With this exceptional navigator's posting there now remained hardly any aircrew on the squadron who belonged to the Hamburg or Peenemunde era of 1943. The squadron, after the devastating losses of autumn and winter, had been virtually forced to reconstitute itself.

The last Berlin raid in the current offensive took place on March 24th. A total of 822 bombers attacked the Big City, using the north-west route out over the North Sea, and so flying for two hours before sighting land. The winds were much stronger than those officially forecast, and the bomber stream was scattered. Some Pathfinder crews could not see any ground markers, and the *Wanganui* flares were drifting wide of the mark in the windy conditions. F/O Gillmore's crew reported that the attack was widespread, Ron Breeze in F/S Cuthill's crew states that 'we dropped our T.Is and *Wanganui* flares on "Y".'

On the return journey many casualties were sustained by aircraft straying into flak belts around the big cities. Aircraft were caught over Leipzig, Magdeburg, Munster, Osnabruck and the Ruhr.

F/S Cuthill, caught like this by the Magdeburg searchlights, dived and twisted around the sky 'like an eel'. Ron Breeze found himself, after coming out of one of these dives, struggling for thirty seconds to pick up an 8 oz packet of paper from the floor, so strong was the gravitational pull. Several Lancasters were observed being shot down in flames over Leipzig and Brunswick by the gunners in F/S Cuthill's crew. And P/O Wadsworth wrote of this raid in his log as follows:

'Coned over Ruhr for fifteen minutes. Aircraft hit by flak, and mid-upper gunner wounded. Very narrow escape.'

F/O Musgrove's wounding that night would save his life, did he but know it.

In many cases those Pathfinder and other crews equipped with H2S were only able to return because of their special equipment. The winds played havoc with many crews, pushed some into the flak bursts, and blew a few off course to crash fatally in the North Sea. One was missing from 156, seventy-three from the whole command. The time for mutual congratulation was over. The missing crew, captained by F/L Richmond, had only been four weeks on the squadron, being posted to 156 on the day the first Stuttgart raid was mounted, February 20th. There was one survivor from this crew, who became a P.O.W.

Two days after the Berlin raid, which, for the Command at large, was the greatest loss of the war to date, came an operation on March 26th. Eleven aircraft from the squadron took off as part of a force of 705 aircraft to bomb Essen. This was a successful raid in every respect. All of the aircraft which set out from Upwood returned after bombing the target, the ten tenths cloud over the target made the defences ineffective, and the fighter force only got their act together after the bombers had left the target. Nine aircraft were missing from the whole of the force.

Nuremberg and After.

At the end of the month came the Nuremberg raid, which is a name which lives in the memory not only of the survivors among the crews who took part, but among all students of aerial warfare. The raid to Nuremberg of March 30th 1944 on the part of 750 aircraft which resulted in ninety-four missing aircraft ranks as the great disaster of the R.A.F. offensive against Germany. It has been the subject of three published books, one of which, by Martin Middlebrook, entitled *The Nuremberg Raid*, was described, in a review in *The Economist*, as the 'best book, whether documentary or fictional, yet written about Bomber Command'. Questions will always be asked as to why the 'straight in–straight out' route was chosen for the raid to Nuremberg, from the east coast straight to

Charleroi, and then a turning and a flight due east for 250 miles. The Group Leader, A/V/M Bennett, questioned the wisdom and appropriateness of the route, only to be overruled, and the bombers set out, twenty of them from Upwood, after one could not proceed because of a burst tyre. It was a bright moonlit night, 'almost as bright as day', the crews said. Scores of German fighters were waiting, and harried the bombers for the whole length of the way. Vigilant gunners gave instructions to their captains to dive or corkscrew, as fighters quite literally queued up to make their passes. Others, not under attack, kept on weaving, diving and turning all the way to the target. Approximately fifty never reached the target. At Upwood the bright moonlight had called forth from the new 'B' flight commander W/C Scott the remark at briefing to the gunners to keep their eyes peeled, as it would be a night fighter night. This was good advice, and all the more pertinent, because it came from the mouth of a former Mosquito night fighter pilot.

Those who did make it to the target found it blanketed in ten tenths cloud. Pathfinders released their flares and bombs by H2S. Attacks by fighters continued all the long journey home, and vapour trails in the intensely cold night highlighted the lumbering bombers, and made their stalking and destruction even more easy than before. Out of 110 Pathfinders twelve failed to return, four of them from Upwood, which sustained the highest loss rate of the Pathfinder squadrons that night, although both Oakington and Downham Market each lost three aircraft.

Two 156 aircraft were shot down by the same German fighter as they flew side by side on the outward journey. Captain F. Johnsen, the Norwegian who had joined the squadron as a 2nd Lieutenant on February 7th, was killed with his crew of seven, including the countryman in his crew, the Norwegian rear gunner, Sgt. Karsman. W/O Jack Murphy, an Australian, was piloting the other aircraft. When it exploded, Sgt. Wooliscroft was flung clear and dropped to earth by parachute to become a P.O.W., the sole survivor from his crew of seven. W/O Murphy and his crew had joined the squadron on January 19th as part of the flood of replacements that poured in that month. They had been on 101 Squadron, which W/C Eaton had once commanded. The Lancaster of P/O Lindley, also of 156, left one survivor, the pilot himself, when he was shot down. Although the crew were on their nineteenth operation together they had not been long on the squadron. From S/L Goodwin's aircraft, another 156 casualty, and his crew of eight, four survived, including the pilot, although he was convinced his hour had come. Trapped in the nose of his Lancaster and spinning down from 18,000 feet he knew he could not get out, and would not have escaped, had not the perspex nose of the aircraft suddenly shattered, enabling him to drag himself through and out. S/L Goodwin had come to Warboys early in January after a period as an instructor at 23 O.T.U., and had got married only six weeks before.

Eleven aircraft of the twenty from Upwood landed at other aerodromes on returning from Nuremberg. As they were making their gradual descent to land at Upwood through apparently impenetrable cloud, crews eventually realised that the cloud was in fact a heavy snowstorm. In one of the eleven diverted aircraft was P/O Wadsworth, flying with a crew of eight in G for George (ND409) piloted on this night by W/C Eaton. His remarks, noted in his log book, indicate a rather average night.

After the Nuremberg raid there was a general stand down for the crews of Bomber Command, an opportunity to lick wounds, replace aircraft, and receive new crews from O.T.Us. Reorganization was afoot no less in 156. On April 1st 156 Squadron lost the aircraft and crews of 'C' flight, which was detached to form a new Pathfinder squadron at Little Staughton. So once again aircraft took off to a new squadron destination, and convoys of trucks made the journey to Little Staughton, not far from St. Neots. The new squadron was designated 582 Squadron, it was made up of one flight ("C" flight) from 156, and another flight from No. 7 Squadron at Oakington. S/L D. M. Walbourn, the 'C' flight commander at this time on 156 Squadron, moved with his flight to Little Staughton. Captain Swales of the S.A.A.F. joined this squadron later and rose to become a flight commander. In February 1945 he won a posthumous V.C. for his action as Master Bomber during an attack on Pforzheim. On April 1st, after the Nuremberg losses of the previous night, it was a depleted 'C' flight that arrived at Little Staughton. The parent squadron at Upwood now operated one establishment of sixteen Lancasters with four in reserve, with numbers of personnel amounting to seventy officers and 378 other ranks. The squadron consisted of two flights, now, rather than the previous three. It was a surgical reduction in size to accommodate an expanding Pathfinder force. The next day, April 2nd, S/L Brooks was granted the acting rank of Wing Commander. He was 'A' flight commander, while W/C Scott remained 'B' flight commander. They would not be with the squadron much longer. Senior commands awaited both of them.

The Berlin battles were now over. Berlin had not, in the words of the memo of Sir Arthur Harris to the Prime Minister defining his ambition the previous autumn, been 'wrecked from end to end', though considerable amounts of damage had been done. Though the loss of crews was punitive, time had run out for the C. in C's ambitions of destroying Berlin to be realised. There would always be more crews; but, in Pathfinders, they could not be trained to the exacting standards required. The one vital and necessary thing Sir Arthur Harris had run out of was time. The invasion of Europe beckoned, and the planning of Operation Overlord required a progressive campaign of dislocation of the enemy's resources and centres of communication near, at, or related to, the Normandy battle front.

Meanwhile 156 Squadron could look back on their efforts since November 1943 with pride as well as sorrow. In the nineteen raids to Berlin they had sent 362 Lancasters to the German capital. The loss rate had been twenty-four aircraft missing, and two aircraft which crashed in England on their return.

Oakington and 7 Squadron suffered a loss rate of twenty-six aircraft missing out of 353 dispatched to Berlin on these raids. So Warboys and later Upwood had the satisfaction of knowing that they had sent more bombers to Berlin than any other Pathfinder Squadron. It was also the case that, though Oakington overtopped 156 Squadron with the figures of lost and missing aircraft, 156 Squadron sustained the greatest overall casualty figures, 168 men killed and eleven P.O.Ws (as compared with Oakington's 146 killed and thirty-nine P.O.Ws.). After the Nuremberg raid, the last operation (so it is reckoned) of the air Battle of Berlin, different considerations dominated the requirements of the planners and tacticians. However much German cities would be pounded in the future, the Berlin dream was over.

Leave came earlier to many 156 crews than was usual. After Nuremberg and the preceding operations the crews needed resting. The squadron's 'slimming down' needed a measure of reorganization and readjustment. By mid-April most crews were back and ready for 'ops'. On April 14th Bomber Command was transferred to the direction of General Eisenhower, which meant that the demands of Overlord predominated over those of the area bombing of German city targets. Thus, from early April, reduced forces of Lancasters attacked railway targets in northern France, Lille on April 9th with six Lancasters, Laon April 10th with seven aircraft, and Rouen on April 18th with fifteen aircraft, all without casualties. On April 11th, by contrast, eleven Lancasters raided Aachen, all of them likewise returning to Upwood. On the night of April 13th the force of sixteen aircraft sent from Upwood were split between two French targets, Rouen, and Noisy-Le-Sec, both of them railway yards. F/O Gillmore and his crew went to Rouen that night, a raid of three and three-quarter hours, where, it was noted, the marker concentration was good. On all these targets good results were obtained at a low cost in casualties to the Command. The great abiding fear was of allied civilian casualties, something which became particularly marked as the Invasion advanced, especially in places like Caen and Le Havre. The C. in C., although he resisted tooth and nail being under General Eisenhower's direction, arguing furthermore that the best way to help the invading forces was to go on bombing German targets, carried out his instructions, once the policy was switched, to the letter with a high degree of flair and skill. This was a new kind of bombing and the crews responded to it. A great onus was placed, of course, upon Pathfinder precision marking. Not only would this avoid civilian casualties, wherever possible, but, as the Invasion advanced, would prevent our own troops from being accidentally bombed.

For three weeks the so-called 'Transportation plan' was energetically pursued by the crews of the Pathfinders and of Bomber Command. On April 20th, however, it was back to the German cities. Cologne was attacked by a force of 357 Lancasters and twenty-two Mosquitoes. No aircraft were lost from the thirteen which set out from Upwood, and four were lost from the whole command. The tide, it was felt, had really turned. The chain of successes was broken two nights later for 156, however, when fourteen aircraft from the squadron visited the French target of Laon yet again on April 22nd. Pathfinders had to go in low to mark these French targets, from heights of between 6,000 and 8,000 feet. The crew of F/S Doyle (a future Master Bomber, who was destined not to survive the war) could not see the green T.Is they had been briefed to bomb. They therefore went round again, a hair raising manoeuvre at that altitude which risked collision, and in the three minutes this took received instructions from the Master Bomber to bomb the centre of the yellow T.Is. F/O Gillmore's report concludes:

'Our bombs were seen to hit aiming point and the whole attack seemed very well concentrated.'

P/O Wadsworth's remarks in his log book echo the general satisfaction:

'Bombed target, illuminated bright as day from 7,500 feet. Bombs hit aiming point. Wizard prang. Very little opposition.'

The crew which failed to return to Upwood that night, that captained by W/O Higgs, had joined 156 only five weeks before. Three members of the crew survived, including the pilot. The feelings and experiences of this crew, on returning from leave, on the morning of March 30th, to find themselves on the battle order on the infamous Nuremberg raid, is described in James Campbell's book, *The Bombing of Nuremberg*. It was hard to go down on a 'moderate' or 'easy' target, as the French targets were supposed to be, after surviving nights when the casualties were prolific, especially for the Pathfinders, but it often happened. W/C Cousens, C.O. of 635 Sqaudron at Downham Market, the Master Bomber on this Laon raid, was shot down and killed. As we shall see, however, at the low level at which they were required to orbit the target, Master Bombers were specially vulnerable on these French targets.

Another German town was visited by our bombers two nights after the Laon raid. This time it was Karlsruhe, and fourteen Lancasters took off from Upwood, bombed and returned. There was little opposition on this raid, it was a well concentrated attack, and all aircraft reported large fires in the target area. In actual fact, when surveys were made after the war, it was found that only the northern part of Karlsruhe was damaged seriously. Nineteen aircraft were lost. W/C Eaton flew that night with a crew which included five of F/O Gillmore's crew, including P/O Wadsworth, and the Squadron Bombing Leader, S/L ('Les') L. H. Glasspool. The C.O. writes in his report:

'Bomb aimer's panel was frosted up, so we did not drop our T.Is but bombed on centre of two T.I. reds. The backing up was very badly spread and T.Is on the ground were going out before they were followed by others. Numerous fires were burning in main area as we left.'

There speaks a C.O. with a concern for exact, precision marking. He had briefed the squadron. He expected results.

The next night operations were cancelled, after fourteen aircraft had been detailed for 'ops', and the following night, April 26th, it was Essen, a return to the old days of the Battle of the Ruhr, although some aircraft raided Villeneuve-St-Georges. From the fourteen aircraft which proceeded that night from Upwood to Essen one failed to return, the Lancaster of F/L Kayll and crew, who had been posted from 7 Squadron on March 1st. Earlier that day, on April 26th, before the Essen raid, the 'A' flight commander, W/C Brooks, and his crew, were posted to Downham Market. W/C Brooks was to be the new C.O. of 635 Squadron, after W/C Cousens, the former C.O., had gone missing from the raid on Laon on April 22nd.

Commanding officers of squadrons were supposed to fly on operations at least once a month with the crews of their squadron. Most of them, however, flew more often than this. The C.O. of 156 was particularly active in this respect. On the next day, April 27th, fourteen aircraft set off from Upwood at 10.00pm., with a different target from the usual run, Friedrichshafen in southern Germany, on the shores of Lake Constance, the German Bodensee on the frontier of Switzerland. The C.O. was flying that night with the crew of F/O Gillmore, the crew he had flown with a number of times before. The difference was that the Squadron Bombing Leader S/L L. H. Glasspool went with W/C Eaton. The Bombing Leader had flown in S/L Walbourn's crew, the former 'C' flight commander, who had gone with his flight to Little Staughton to form the new squadron. So it was appropriate that he should fly with another senior pilot.

Friedrichshafen, which housed the old Zeppelin sheds, was a town which manufactured aircraft (there were Dornier factories), tank engines, gearboxes for tanks and radar equipment, extending to components for the V2 rockets. To attack this town was part of the plan to hit the German fighter and tank replacements just before the Invasion, and to hit out against the German V2 programme. The force which set out numbered 322, with most of them coming from 1 Group. The target was famous in the annals of Bomber Command, as, when it was last attacked, on June 20th 1943, by over sixty Lancasters, the Master Bomber technique had been used for the first time. The June 1943 raid had largely been a 5 Group show, with four Pathfinder aircraft from 97 Squadron adding their expertise. Another novel feature of this raid was that the attacking bombers flew on to North Africa, and confused the German fighters waiting along the return route. Thus, remarkably even so, there were no casualties.

The same cannot be said for the Friedrichshafen raid of April 1944,. The target was deep in southern Germany, and it was another bright moonlit night, a good night fighter night, like Nuremberg four weeks before. Indeed the trip to Friedrichshafen was longer. However, a number of other things were happening that night. Raids took place also on two other targets, Aulnoye (223 aircraft) and Montzen (144 aircraft), twenty four Mosquitoes provided a diversionary raid to Stuttgart, and 159 aircraft from the O.T.Us conducted a lengthy diversionary sweep over the North Sea. So the fighter controllers did not identify the Friedrichshafen target until the bombers had arrived.

This was a raid which was described by the C. in C. as an outstanding success, with good Pathfinder marking, minimum 'creep-back', and every one of the six vital factories destroyed. The Master Bomber, S/L Cresswell, of 35 Squadron at Graveley, controlled the bombing. He had been Deputy Master Bomber on the Nuremberg raid, and knew his business. This was a raid, however, which developed very differently. Various natural features at or near the target enabled crews to see what was going on. Crews spoke of how it was the most beautiful target they had visited. The bomb run took aircraft directly towards the Alps, and the snow of the mountains and the reflections in Lake Constance, with first green T.Is and then red T.Is going down, provided a kaleidoscopic pattern of shimmering reflections. F/L Ison reports:

'Bomb aimer had a good view of lake and clearly saw the docks to south of aiming point, and the tip of the wood and the position of the aiming point pinpointed between them. At first, the attack overshot, but later came well back on the aiming point by the time of our own bombs at 0203 hours. A good explosion at about 0210 hours appeared near the Zeppelin shed.'

This vivid report reflects the concern for accuracy, economy and effectiveness that was to lead 'Tiny' Ison along the road to becoming a Master Bomber himself, and ultimately C.O. of the squadron.

Over the target itself and on the approaches and exits the sky was thick with fighter flares. Eighteen Lancasters were lost. Some main force squadrons lost heavily on this raid: Kirmington (166 Squadron) lost four, and so did Mildenhall, two from each of the squadrons it housed (15 Squadron and 622 Squadron). Other fenland locations lost bombers, one from Mepal and one from Witchford. Three Pathfinder aircraft failed to return from Friedrichshafen, one from Graveley (35 Squadron), while both Oakington and Upwood lost their C.Os and their crews that night.

I have dwelt on this raid, its circumstances and losses, because of my personal interest in it. My father, F/O Philip Wadsworth, (he was gazetted as F/O posthumously) was, of course, W/C Eaton's flight engineer, as he had been when the C.O. had flown with this crew several times previously. There were five D.F.Cs in the crew, with the presence of the C.O. and the Squadron Bombing Leader making it, in contemporary parlance, a 'gen' crew. They had survived, all of them, more difficult targets, and more crippling rates of attrition, and they had an enormous number of operations to their credit, as a collective total. Despite the fact that many crews had known worse, the raid on Friedrichshafen of April 1944, with eighteen missing out of 322, 5.6 per cent of 322, only a part of the bomber force (remember the diversions and alternative targets) went down, as I have learned from some former aircrew, as a 'shaky do'. Just as P/O Philip Wadsworth became F/O posthumously so W/C Eaton became Group Captain. His wife wrote to the wives and parents of the rest of the crew, and kept them in touch with news, and developments. It was not for some time that the bodies of the crew were formally and positively identified, and as is the way with official notifications, and procedures, death was then officially confirmed. The plight and dilemma of the women who wait and hope, who are the real and unofficial heroines of this narrative (and there were thousands and thousands of them), is something which filtered down to me through the period of boyhood, and youth and beyond. It has indeed, as I have indicated, been responsible for my wish to search out and write down as much as I could of this period.

The hopes and false trails of widows and the information and misinformation fed to them is conveyed also in a book published in 1979 entitled *Missing in Action: May-September 1944*, by Peggy Ryle. The book consists of a series of letters written by Mrs. Peggy Ryle to her missing husband, S/L George Ryle, confiding her thoughts and hopes and fears from the time when she received the news that her husband was missing on that Friday morning, April 28th, until the Red Cross authorities were able to announce the identification of the bodies the following September. The book was published after her daughter thirty-five years later found a trunk of her mother's letters on cleaning out an attic. S/L George Ryle was in the Pathfinder aircraft that failed to return to Oakington from Friedrichshafen on the same night that the C.O. of 156 Squadron also perished with my father in the crew. S/L Ryle was rear gunner of the aircraft. He had been on 156 Squadron for a short time, and was posted from Warboys after the Peenemunde raid in August 1943, to 7 Squadron at Oakington, one of those sideways postings from Pathfinder station to Pathfinder station that we have heard so much about already. When he flew to Friedrichshafen he was Squadron Gunnery Leader, and his pilot was the C.O. of 7 Squadron, W/C Guy Lockhart, D.S.O., D.F.C. and Bar, an extraordinary figure, legendary among C.Os. He had flown in Lysanders with the 'secret squadrons' from Tangmere and Tempsford earlier in the war to pick up and put down agents, he had been shot down, had escaped over the Spanish border, escaped from a Spanish internment camp, returned to England, and had commanded 692 Squadron, a Mosquito Pathfinder Squadron at Graveley, for a short time. After the death in action of 7 Squadron's C.O., G/C Rampling, on March 22nd over Frankfurt, W/C Lockhart became C.O. of 7 Squadron on March 24th. He lasted just one month, which was not quite as long as his successor, the brilliant New Zealander W/C Fraser Barron, D.S.O., D.F.C., D.F.M, who lasted three weeks, and took command of 7 Squadron from the Friedrichshafen raid until he collided with his Deputy Master Bomber in a raid upon the railway yards at Le Mans on May 20th. Both were from 7 Squadron. Both were killed.

Many crews shot down over southern Germany including those just mentioned, from 7 Squadron, are buried in the beautiful war cemetery of Durnbach in the Tegernsee area of Germany, near to the Austrian border. G/C Eaton, D.F.C., lies there in a row of seven headstones (crews were buried together as crews wherever possible), and alongside him his crew of that night, S/L L. H. Glasspool D.F.C., J.R. Dodds, D.F.C., F/O P. Wadsworth, F/O K. O. Franklin,

D.F.C., F/L C. A. Kidd, and F/O R. G. Sharland, D.F. C. My father was twenty-two years old, and I was ten months.

The successor C.O. at Upwood was W/C T. L. Bingham-Hall, D.F.C. who commanded 156 until a posting on November 21st, 1944, retiring from command as a Group Captain with a D.S.O. to add to his D.F.C. His successor, W/C D. B. Falconer, D.F.C., A.F.C. took command of 156 that day, and was killed just over five weeks later, when 1944 had but one more day to go, over Cologne. Squadron commanding officers led from the front, and their lives were not long.

After the shock of losing the C.O. on the raid of April 27th, a trip by fourteen aircraft of the squadron to bomb railway yards at the French town of Somain made a welcome change from the severity of a German target. As we shall see, however, the French targets were to prove increasingly no soft option, and some of the finest crews of 156 and other Pathfinder squadrons were to end their lives bombing them.

Durnbach war cemetery: grave of G/C Eaton and crew.   (*Taff Jones*)

Taff and Norah Jones.   *(Taff Jones)*

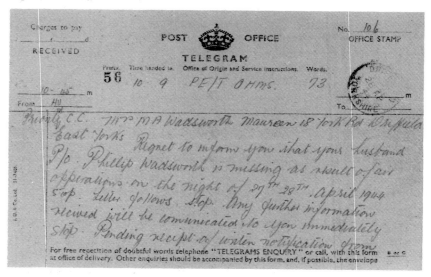

The telegram.   *(Mrs. Margaret Wadsworth)*

CHAPTER 7

UPWOOD AND OVERLORD

'After you, Claude.'
'No, after you, Cecil.'

(Conversation between two bomber pilots on the R.T.,
overheard during a daylight operation, as the target
was approached. The exchange owes something to the
popular radio I.T.M.A. programme)

The Move to Upwood

R.A.F. Upwood was one of those permanent peace time stations that war time aircrew dreamed of inhabiting. It had been in existence as an R.A.F. aerodrome for two years before the outbreak of war. Airmen's married quarters, Warrant Officers' married quarters, Officers' married quarters were all laid out, and were occupied by those whom a peace time airforce intended them for. With the coming of war all this changed. One day before war was declared families were evacuated from their quarters. Upwood received its flights of Fairey Battles. These were not long on the airfield, and having been used in a training capacity, left the station in early 1940. Following the Battles were Blenheim Is of 35 Squadron and 90 Squadron, and Blenheim bomber training began in earnest. This was the pattern at Upwood until April 1943, from which point an ambitious programme of runway construction and adaptation began in readiness for the Halifaxes and Lancasters of the Pathfinder N.T.U. (Navigational Training Unit). Even so, with reconstruction taking place alongside training, R.A.F. Upwood was not ready for use, without depending upon the generous facilities of Warboys, until November 1943, which was only a short hop to February 1944 when 139 Squadron moved to Upwood from Warboys, as part of the Pathfinder Light Night Striking Force, and March 1944, when the Lancasters of 156 Squadron arrived, after which the Pathfinder N.T.U. moved, of course, to Warboys. Ron Smith in his book *Rear Gunner Pathfinders* describes the displacement and dislocation for a crew joining 156 at this time. At the end of 1943 F/S Jack Cuthill and his crew moved from 626 Squadron to the N.T.U. at Upwood. Ron Breeze, flight engineer in the crew at this time, makes the period of stay at the N.T.U. from January 9th 1944 until January 19th, when a move to Warboys and 156 Squadron occurred, and, characteristically an operation to Berlin on the afternoon of the next day. Six weeks later, there came the move to Upwood. Ron Smith, rear gunner in F/S Cuthill's crew, mentions that the move cheered everybody; it was good to exchange the long nissen huts for pre-war married quarters, while officers lived in enviable comfort, with central heating, constant hot and cold water, batwomen ('they batted better', my father remarked to my mother), and an Officers' Mess that was palatial. You can see this Officers' Mess if you take the little road to the aerodrome from Bury, and drive past the expansion of post-war housing in a ribbon development all along the narrow road. At the gates of the aerodrome, now occupied by the U.S.A.F., you can see the guardroom, the Station Headquarters, and the Sergeants' Mess, with the Officers' Mess set back behind lawns with gently spreading trees to the fore and accessible to the main road through a separate entrance. In pre-war times the station's roses used to win prizes in flower shows in the area. A stroll around the aerodrome, if you can obtain the necessary permission, and make the leap of imagination required, will show you how it all was, married quarters, little semi-detached houses, and blocks of barracks taken over by aircrew and other personnel, all grouped around the parade ground. At the back of this complex of buildings, and to the north, stood the four 'C' type hangars, three of them in a row, and one behind. You can see these hangars clearly for miles from the roads from March and Peterborough, as the ground to the north rises up to the airfield, sitting there on its own plateau. Beyond the airfield stood the control tower, demolished in the 1960s, while the runways, in a flurry of intersections, shoot out north to south, west to east, and south-west to north-east, to be caught up by a perimeter track, from which aircraft would taxi back into their pans (there were ten of these) or those more generous rhomboid hardstandings (of which there were thirty). As well as the control tower, the runways, along which the Lancasters roared, have mostly been removed. Far to the north-west, well away from domestic habitation, or public roads, yet not too far from part of the perimeter track, was the Bomb Store, to the outward eye a complex of dugouts with chains and lifting tackle lying about like basking snakes. To the south and west of the airfield, with its own little lost road meandering through it, stood the villlage of Upwood, with an ancient church, and a seventeenth century manor house, Upwood House.

The people of Upwood were warm people and welcoming, as those of Warboys had been, although the village was on a much smaller scale. Many friendships and relationships had been made in Warboys, and these, of course, were not left behind. The bicycles still went in to Warboys, and for newcomers to the squadron, and for others, the fenland town of Ramsey, north east of the airfield, and on the road from Warboys, was an additional place to be visited. Peterborough was that bit nearer, and airmen and airwomen (we must not forget the W.A.A.Fs) explored the small communities along the fens of the old

Bedford river, that smooth straight, lazy canal which was a natural compass and indicator to aircrew returning to their home fields, whenever they flew in, from a north German target, over the Wash.

The first few weeks at Upwood were dogged by losses. There were the losses of the Nuremberg raid of March 30th (four from Upwood out of a total from the Command of 94). Three other crews went missing in the rest of March and April, while on April 27th the C.O., W/C Eaton, went missing. May was a time of bombing French targets, especially rocket launching sites, centres of communication, and, occasionally (although this became increasingly common after the Invasion started) troop concentrations. The squadron sent fourteen aircraft to Mailly-le-Camp on May 3rd, to bomb a German military camp, and all returned safely, although the Command had a bad night with forty-two aircraft lost. A little after this it was, justifiably, decided that a French target did not count one third of an 'op', as it had done up to then, but the value of an entire operation. St. Ghislain had been bombed on the first day of May, and its railway yards utterly devastated. Mantes-la-Julie was bombed three days after Mailly, and this time F/L H. W. Churchill, D.F.C. and crew did not get back. This gallant captain and crew, posted to the squadron on February 20th, had to go on an 'easy' one, on a target which cost the 149 aircraft which set out two Lancasters and one Halifax. They had stayed the average period of duration for any aircrew member on 156, and during that time the captain had been awarded his D.F.C., as well as one other crew member, and another one had won the D.F.M., and the crew had been to some of the toughest and costliest targets in Germany and occupied Europe. F/L Churchill perished at the controls of his Lancaster, allowing four of his crew to bale out. A few days later he received a Bar to his D.F.C.

On May 7th the squadron received a new C.O. to succeed W/C Eaton. W/C T. L. Bingham-Hall, D.F.C. arrived, and that very night fourteen aircraft bombed the airfield at Nantes, and all came back. In a raid on Hasselt on May 11th the squadron battled it out with night fighters. F/L J. 't. Hart, a Lancaster pilot from the Netherlands, was attacked by a fighter just as he was leaving the target. The Master Bomber had broadcast instructions to return with the bombs. In flames and with a full bomb load, the Lancaster struggled on, and the pilot had to put the aircraft into a dive that nearly pulled the wings off in order to extinguish the fire. In the meanwhile the rear and mid-upper gunners had baled out over enemy occupied territory. F/L J. 't. Hart landed the aircraft at Woodbridge with the remaining members of his crew. P/O Griffin's aircraft was attacked by an ME210, and the rear gunner was wounded. He made his way back to Upwood to find that he had to be diverted to Warboys. At Upwood the runway was blocked by the Lancaster of S/L Davies, D.S.O. In an attack on his aircraft by an enemy fighter one of his aircraft's tyres had been punctured. In the attempt to land at Upwood one of the tyres of S/L Davies' aircraft had caught fire. As all the aircraft had been instructed to bring back their bombs, the runway was temporarily unuseable, as the Lancaster that had just skated across the runway with its tyre on fire had a full bomb load on board. Fortunately firetenders dealt effectively with the blaze. In a raid to a German target, Duisburg, on May 21st, F/S Ward and his crew did not return. With this crew, which had only recently joined the squadron, there perished the Squadron Gunnery Officer, S/L J. F. Blair, D.F.C., D.F.M., who flew with them as rear gunner. He had done sixty-six operations.

F/S Ralph Temple also had a hectic time over Duisburg on the night of May 21st. After his aircraft had bombed and left the target area, they were attacked by a JU88. The rear gunner, Sgt. W. V. Cooper and the mid-upper, Sgt. L. E. Reynolds, drove off their attacker with accurately returned fire. Just then a second enemy fighter, an ME110, dived down on the stricken Lancaster. Sgt. Reynolds, suffering from a head and neck wound caused in the earlier attack continued to man his turret, with the result that, because of excellent team work between the two gunners, this second aircraft also was driven off.

Now began the aircraft's own private fight. The Lancaster had been left in a desperately poor condition. The starboard elevator had been shot away, as well as the port rudder. The rudder trimmers and elevator were unserviceable. There was no oxygen in the mid-upper and rear turrets. Gee and H2S were useless, and the starboard main plane and the fuselage were a mass of holes. With the aircraft barely responding, Ralph Temple directed it in the opposite direction from the flak. Even then an engine burst into flames after a very unsteady flight of one hour. Luckily the fire did not engulf the aircraft, and subsided. Going on and ever on through apparently impenetrable cloud, the crew noticed lights below them. They did not know it at the time but they were over Guildford railway station. Orbiting slowly this source of light to indicate his distress, Ralph Temple saw searchlights switched on, and then the search-lights sweeping flatly beam on to point him to the nearest available place to land, which happened to be R.A.F. Dunsfold. The landing was difficult. There was no brake pressure, and the aircraft smashed through several obstructions to be brought to a halt by a pile of tree roots removed previously by bulldozer to make ready for a lengthened runway. There were Dutch airmen at Dunsfold, and they pulled out the crew from their burning Lancaster. Sgt. Reynolds, the mid-upper gunner, who stayed at his post with serious wounds, received an immediate D.F.M. Not long afterwards Ralph Temple was commissioned, and ended the war as a flight lieutenant with a D.F.C., to which was added an M.B.E., and a Polish M.C. He is a past President of the Pathfinder Association, and is often to be seen at squadron reunions.

Master Bombers and Army Support

During this month of May there were one or two German targets attacked. As well as Duisburg there was Dortmund a night later (May 22nd) and Aachen was attacked twice. In addition to those operations already mentioned, there were the nights when the squadron divided itself into two, and, while one section bombed a special radar installation in northern France (of sufficient sensitivity, in intelligence terms, to be called 'Special Target' in the *Operations Record Book*) another section attacked marshalling yards (May 19th). On the last day of May P/O Taggart, an Australian pilot from 156, carried out the duties of Master Bomber in a raid on Tergnier, while another crew in the squadron, captained by S/L M. R. Attwater, acted as Deputy Master Bomber. On this raid F/L Samson, an Australian pilot, and his crew failed to return. He and three other crew members managed to escape from the burning Lancaster, and 'Sammy' Samson joined the French Maquis, until he was returned to this country, arriving back at Upwood and the squadron in August. He had received his promotion to Acting Flight Lieutenant the day he went missing.

On the first day of June a postgram came from Pathfinder Headquarters granting the previous C.O., W/C Eaton, D.F.C., missing since the attack on Friedrichshafen on April 27/28th, the acting rank of Group Captain, with effect from February 4th. Sadly, as I have already indicated, this increase in rank, though it was not known at the time, was posthumous. There was now a worrying away at important French communication targets, and rail links. It was known, on both sides of the Channel, that invasion was in the air. On May 3rd nine Upwood Lancasters bombed Calais coastal batteries, and on the 5th the batteries at Houlgate and Langues were pounded, with sixteen aircraft from 156 taking part. On the night of the invasion, June 6th, Bomber Command made a maximum all-out attack on French railway and road centres just behind the Normandy battle area. In this maximum effort 1,065 aircraft of the Command were involved. Thirteen aircraft from Upwood were detailed, and were later scrubbed. There were two exceptions, however. S/L Godfrey, D.F.C. and S/L Ison had been briefed for the roles of Master Bomber and Deputy Master Bomber, respectively, and flew off to fulfil that function over the target of Achères. Because of thick cloud over this target, the Master Bomber ordered the mission to be aborted. Casualties to French civilians might be inevitable, but extreme care had to be taken because of this eventuality, and on account of the proximity of our troops, as the battle lines advanced. During the following night (June 7th), in a raid on railhead connections at Versailles 156 squadron lost an experienced Canadian pilot and flight commander, S/L Hopton, D.F.C. and his crew, who were acting as Deputy Master Bomber, while S/L Ison was Master Bomber, and F/O Wiseman, D.F.C., Visual Backer Up. As the crew's radar operator, F/L R. B. Leigh, was sick at the time, F/L D. T. Wood, D.F.C., the Squadron Bombing Leader, took his place, and perished with the crew. Two targets were attacked on the night of June 9th, Le Mans, and Rennes. On their return flight the Lancaster of P/O Ribbins was damaged by light flak and the port inner engine burst into flames. The crippled aircraft was hit a second time by flak, causing fire to break out in the starboard inner engine. Both engines were feathered, and the flames extinguished. In order not to bring calamity upon the airfield and themselves, and to use up remaining fuel, P/O Ribbins circled Upwood until all the other crews had been interrogated and had gone off to bed. He then brought the badly damaged Lancaster in to a perfect landing on three engines, with a punctured port tyre. W/C Burroughs also landed on three engines that night.

At this time 156 Squadron was coming into its own as the Pathfinder Squadron to produce Master Bombers and Deputy Master Bombers. Master Bombers and their Deputies over the French targets were required to display a great deal of precision, to fly low and to remain circling the target. Over the next few months, again and again, these skilled and courageous captains and crews came from 156. On June 11th in an attack on Tours marshalling yards F/L Taggart was Master Bomber, while S/L Attwater was his Deputy. F/L Taggart was Master Bomber again on June 14th in a raid on the St. Pol Station area, while F/O R. C. Wiseman D.F.C. was Deputy Master Bomber. On June 21st occurred the squadron's first 'daylight'. On this, a raid on one of the flying bomb sites at St. Martin-l'Hortier, bombed through ten tenths cloud, S/L T. E. Ison was Master Bomber, and S/L M. R. Attwater Deputy Master Bomber, while, on a raid on Bientanes on June 23rd, the Master Bomber was S/L Attwater (now awarded the D.F.C), and S/L Godfrey, D.F.C. acted as his Deputy. That same day fourteen aircraft from 156 took part in an attack on another flying bomb location at Coubronnes, and P/O Langford and his crew failed to return. The Flight Engineer Leader, F/L R. E. Manvell, D.F.C., D.F.M., was flying in the missing Lancaster. On June 27th we find S/L Godfrey D.F.C. has moved from being Deputy to acting in the capacity of Master Bomber, with S/L G. G. Davies, D.S.O. as Deputy. Only these two aircraft left Upwood, and directed 104 Halifaxes of 4 Group, and five Mosquitoes in yet another raid on a V-weapon site, at Mimoyecques. Two French targets were also attacked by the squadron that night. It was a period of intense activity, this immediate post-invasion time, with day and night operations calling forth supreme and heroic 'round the clock' efforts on the part of ground crews. The last French target of this 'invasion' month of June was Donleger, a flying bomb site on the 29th, with F/L Wiseman D.F.C. as Master Bomber and F/L 't. Hart, D.F.C. as Deputy. F/L Wiseman brought his Lancaster home riddled by flak. The Deputy Master Bomber from the Netherlands, F/L 't. Hart, had been decorated 'in the field' when A/C Don Bennett, the Commander of Pathfinder Force, had visited Upwood on June 20th and given him the D.F.C. personally. F/L t'. Hart and his crew had only been posted to the squadron two months before this meteoric rise of their captain to Deputy Master Bomber and the award of the D.F.C. This 'invasion' month had been a series of French targets, with only one German target, Gelsenkirchen, raided by only three Lancasters of 156 on June 12th, without loss to themselves.

July began with more attacks on flying bomb sites, 'ski sites' in aircrew parlance. Once more 156 Squadron provided two Lancasters for the Master Bomber (captained by S/L Godfrey, D.F.C) and for the Deputy (F/L t'. Hart

D.F.C), during this daylight raid on St. Martin-l'Hortier. The next day, July 2nd, the rocket platforms in Oisemont were raided.

The crew of P/O Cuthill had not taken part in the squadron's first 'daylight' on June 21st. Oisemont was, therefore, their first daylight raid. Ron Breeze, the flight engineer in the crew, writes of the strange sensation of seeing everything take place around you, in the air and on the ground, especially after being wedded to the night for so long:

'the target was the concrete works for launching 'Doodlebugs', situated on the edge of a wood somewhere in France . . . Although I could see bombs bursting everywhere, the target was not identifiable until we were very nearly on top of it. The bombers in front of us had dropped their bombs in the woods, along a road. I followed them down, and saw them blow up clouds of earth and bricks. Some people were seen running in the fields, but they did not get far. I think they were German soldiers. We turned off the target and started back, and on our starboard side a plane was hit by flak and started burning as it went down. It left a trail of black smoke in the sky.'

All sixteen Upwood aircraft returned from this raid. W/O Clarke, a pilot who had acquitted himself bravely during the time he had been with 156, and who had been awarded the D.F.M., crashed on return, with some slight injury to two of his crew. That same day six Upwood Lancasters were made ready for a night operation which was later cancelled. There was a night operation on the 5th when V-1 launching sites and storage sites were attacked. The squadron's contribution was to provide a Master Bomber, F/L Taggart (who had led some attacks last month and had now been awarded the D.F.C), and S/L Attwater, D.F.C. as Deputy, to lead the attack on Biennais. The next night but one, one of 156 Squadron's regular 'teams', S/L Ison as Master Bomber, and F/L Wiseman, D.F.C. as Deputy, led the attack on the marshalling yards at Vaires. The list of targets this month can be divided into railway or communication centres, as a part of General Eisenhower's transportation plan (note the Americanism), or battlefield targets, as the Normandy front advanced, with the 'blockages' being bombed ahead of the forward troops, or 'ski-sites', mobile or permanent rocket launching pads, camouflaged or blanketed by woods in and around the Pas de Calais area.

On the day that the pair from 156 led the attack on the marshalling yards at Vaires, W/O Clarke, D.F.M. ended his tour, while F/L J. A. Wilson took over his crew. But that was not all. The tough Australian Master Bomber, F/L Taggart, D.F.C., also ended his tour. These were happy events, and the men of 156 watched the odds lengthen, and felt that, perhaps, after all, they might survive the war, something barely considered on the squadron five months before when the Berlin losses were at their height.

Six launching sites were raided on July 9th. Eight Lancasters from Upwood raided L'Hey, while two, S/L Attwater, D.F.C., in partnership with S/L Davies, D.S.O., as Master and Deputy respectively, led an attack on Chateau Bernapre.

Another launching site was the subject of a raid the following day, with fourteen Upwood Lancasters going to Nucourt, while the next day, July 11th, three separate battle orders were issued for daylight raids. The first was against a flying bomb site at Gapennes, a precision attack with W/C Somerville of Pathfinder Headquarters as Master Bomber. Seven aircraft took part from Upwood. The second attack was again on Gapennes and was distinguished from the many others which preceded it by being directed by the pilot of a Lancaster fitted with Oboe. It was thus the first 'heavy Oboe' attack, and the Master Bomber directing the raid was W/C G. F. Grant, D.S.O., D.F.C. who had been with 156 Squadron until he was posted to Pathfinder Headquarters in November 1943. This exceptional pilot was now commanding 109 Mosquito Squadron at Little Staughton, and he was flying in a specially converted Lancaster of 582 Squadron from the same station. Shortly after the move to Upwood by 156 Squadron, 'C' flight was detached to make up this new Squadron at Little Staughton. In December of this year, 1944, G/C (as he became) Grant would find himself Station Commander at Graveley.

In between these two raids on Gapennes six crews were awaiting take-off when the operation was scrubbed. So there had been, as already indicated, three battle orders on July 11th. Three battle orders followed on the next day, July 12th, and all of them were carried out, a 'daylight' on Rollez (a rocket platform) by six aircraft, one against a flying bomb storage dump by five aircraft, and last of all a night raid on Tours marshalling yards.

The Rollez trip, Ron Breeze recalls, was fairly trouble free. Three Pathfinder Squadrons, including 156, had sent six aircraft each to Rollez with each group of six being led by an Oboe-equipped Mosquito. The Lancasters flew in tight formation following the Oboe Mosquito, and the bomb release was pressed as soon as the Mosquito's bombs were seen to fall. The target was covered with thick cloud, and no flak or fighters were observed. Through gaps in the clouds on the return journey thousands of bomb craters could be seen in the open fields.

This period of sure-footed, smoothly executed operations was bound to come to an end sooner or later. The next night but one, July 14th, a raid on the Revigny marshalling yards in southern France, was a "hot" one for the crews of 156. After a 'ski-site' attack during the day in thick cloud by six Làncasters of 156 against St. Philibert Ferme, with no casualties, nine aircraft took off from Upwood for a night raid on Revigny. F/L R. C. Wiseman, D.F.C. was Master Bomber and S/L G. G. Davies, D.S.O., was Deputy. Take off was at 10.00pm. still in daylight. It was a long haul to southern France, as the crews had been instructed to use a roundabout route. As the aircraft approached the target, Ron Breeze recalls that, in the light of the flares, he could clearly see the railway lines and locomotive sheds. 'But the Master Bomber was shot down,' Ron Breeze writes, 'as he was going to mark the target. After going around three times, the target was still unmarked, and so we were ordered to return to base with our bombs.'

In fact it was the Deputy Master Bomber whom Ron Breeze had seen shot down, S/L Davies of 156. The Master Bomber F/L Wiseman lived to fight another day, and indeed to complete a distinguished tour. The Deputy Master Bomber S/L Davies, and one other member of his crew of eight survived. The Master Bomber F/L Wiseman reports that he made three runs over the target. Having identified the aiming point on the first run, the flares he had called for were very widespread, so that on the second run at 4,000 feet he could no longer identify the aiming point. Going down to 2,000 feet for a third run over the target, the Master Bomber again could not make an identification. Having spoken to the Deputy at 0153 hours, and being told that he could not identify, the Master Bomber gave the code word for 'Abandon Mission'. Just after that, the Deputy was shot down. Like several operations on the railway or rocket targets there was no flak or searchlights. The Master Bomber, however, reported considerable fighter activity over the target area. Ron Breeze describes how his crew were chased by one fighter, just after leaving the target. Having dodged this fighter, the crew ran into another two. 'We twisted around like eels,' Ron says, 'at one time turning right around and starting back for the target. This foxed them, and they left us. By this time the fighter pack had got into the stream of bomb-laden bombers, and were playing havoc. Lancasters burst into flames all over the sky. I saw eight burning.'

French targets were not always, or by any means, 'milk runs'. Seven Lancasters were lost on this raid to Revigny. Missing with the crew of the Deputy Master Bomber was the Squadron Bombing Leader, F/L K. Stevens, although both he and the pilot survived to become P.O.Ws, having been blown out of the aircraft when it exploded. A popular squadron character who perished in this aircraft missing from Revigny was a Belgian flight engineer P/O F. C. G. DeBrock, known as 'the Count', who came to the squadron following a spell as engineer leader with No. 101 Squadron, Ludford Magna, the squadron W/C Eaton used to command.

The next day saw two attacks, one 'daylight', one night raid. The 'daylight' (with six Upwood aircraft) was to Nucourt on a flying bomb supply dump, with Oboe Mosquitoes leading. S/L Godfrey was Master Bomber, and the intrepid Netherlander F/L J. t'Hart his Deputy. That night two Lancasters from 156 Squadron joined in a precision raid on a rocket-launching site at Bois-des-Jardins. On July 17th the squadron supplied two Master Bomber and Deputy 'pairs', S/L Attwater, D.F.C., (M.B) and F/L A. W. G. Cochrane, D.F.C.,(D.M.B) for a raid on Mont Condon, and S/L Godfrey, D.F.C.(M.B) and F/L J. N. McDonald (D.M.B) for a raid on Bois de la Haie, both of these being daylight operations on flying bomb sites.

The raid on July 18th during the day to Caen and its surrounding villages, which were about to be attacked by the British Second Army troops, was a classic of its kind. The raid was on five distinct targets in the Caen area, and twelve Upwood Lancasters were taking part. The total force was 942 bombers. One aircraft of the 156 Lancasters was to attack Cagny, one Caen North, one Caen South, one Mannerville, and one Sommerville. Ron Breeze's crew, captained by P/O Cuthill, was to attack Cagny. Take off was at 4.40am., into an East Anglian dawn. Climbing up to 5,000 feet the course was set down the country, diverting past London and out over Normandy. All the time the sky was packed with reverberating Lancasters and Halifaxes. After successfully bombing the target, Ron Breeze saw, on the return, a heavy barrage being laid down by British battleships lying off shore. Air and naval mastery was demonstrated to a supreme extent, and crews, as they returned, sensed that an allied victory was assured. P/O Cuthill's crew was cock-a-hoop, with an aiming point photograph.

There was no rest for the Cuthill crew, however. After the three hour flight to Cagny and back, 'ops' were on again that night with Wesseling as the target. Not that this was a traditional 'area' attack, for the aiming point was a synthetic oil factory on the bank of the river. Whereas the Cagny raid saw the crew take off just as dawn was breaking, the take-off to Wesseling was at 23.10 hours, just as darkness was falling. Five Lancasters took off for Wesseling, and four for Scholven, another synthetic oil plant. The Cuthill crew acted as Blind Marker Illuminators over Wesseling. The barrage over the target was intense and concentrated. This was truly a return to previous conditions. 'The barrage was very heavy', Ron Breeze records, 'and several bursts came very near us, too near. We were weaving like a fish, and dropped our delayed action bombs and flares. Then we got out of there as fast as we could. It was pretty hot all the while, and we were the only aircraft over at the time. It took us fifteen minutes to get away from there. After we left, the rest of the boys were over and they were lighting it up. Our flares had dropped right on the river'.

When the crews reached Upwood three and a half hours after take-off, they had trouble landing. When they examined their old M for Mother, when her wheels had finally come to rest, they discovered an aerial shot away, and a big hole torn in the right rudder. One piece of shrapnel had landed in the front turret, just one foot from the flight engineer's head. Fortunately for 156, this had been a casualty-free day and night, for all the grim and hair-raising experiences of P/O Cuthill and his crew.

The next two days saw further attacks on flying-bomb sites, and V-weapon sites. A 'daylight' on July 19th to Rollez was followed, the next day, by a raid by eight aircraft to Foret du Croc, although on this raid the controlling Mosquito leader found his equipment to be unserviceable, and the force could not bomb. On the night of July 20th on a raid to a flying-bomb site at Anderbeck, S/L Godfrey was Master Bomber, while an extremely competent and popular Australian pilot, F/O Ken Doyle, was Deputy. Ken Doyle had been pilot of a Lancaster to Berlin on February 15th, when F/S A. G. Smith, a fellow Australian, who was the aircraft's rear gunner, had won the Conspicuous Gallantry Medal for remaining at his turret even though severely wounded, so severely that his right leg had had to be amputated.

The relentless pounding of the 'ski sites' went on. Coulanvilles on July 22nd was raided, with an Oboe Mosquito leading. The next day there was a 'daylight' by eight Upwood Lancasters on Foret-du-Croc, with two night operations, S/Ls Godfrey and Doyle acting as Master Bomber and Deputy against Les Catelliers (a 'ski-site'), and S/Ls Ison and Attwater acting in the same capacity against Donges Oil Refinery. Sixteen aircraft from Upwood attacked Les Catelliers, while fourteen attacked Donges. Spectacular, coruscating explosions were observed by crews who bombed the oil refinery, as the huge tanks went up in flames. The strange variety of this July month was demonstrated by the events of the next two days, when flying bomb sites were bombed in the daytime (Acquet on the 24th, Coquereaux on the 25th), while Stuttgart was raided during the night. S/Ls Attwater and Slade were Master Bomber and Deputy against Coquereaux. Stuttgart suffered three heavy raids in five nights, the two in which 156 Squadron took part being on July 24th and 25th, with a third on July 28th, in which, under a bright moon, thirty-nine Lancasters were shot down. On the night of the third Stuttgart raid 156 Squadron sent sixteen aircraft to Hamburg. F/L R. C. Wiseman, D.F.C., (with seventy operations), S/L T. W. Godfrey, D.F.C. (with sixty-one) and S/L H. F. Slade (with fifty-eight) all finished their tours in this Hamburg raid, in the case of Fred Slade in a spectacular way. To convey the horror and excitement of that night for S/L Slade and his crew, I append now the entry he made in the *Operations Record Book* of 156 Squadron, without any amendment or abridgement. He writes as follows:

'*Sustained direct hit by flak on port main plane trailing edge from the spar back, a fraction before bombing. Went on and dropped bombs and went into a slow spiral out of control. Captain ordered crew to Grab parachutes and stand by to jump. Then said, Still out of control, don't panic, plenty of height, 17,000 ft. Stand BY Captain observed that port wing had broken upwards, almost size of tail fin and rudder, obviously causing great turbulence at speed (190 knots) at which we were descending. I had elevator control, and managed to lift nose and bring speed back to 155 knots, still in spiral. I applied coarse right rudder, extra power on port side (2650 plus 8) and with rudder and motor, lifted aircraft on to even keel, still without aileron control. Ordered engineer back to check engine temperatures, fuel capacity, etc. Notified navigator that I had much difficulty in turning to port and to ask him to give early notification of turns in that direction, which he did, bringing me out of target on wide turn. Navigator and engineer showed coolness and courage. On reaching enemy coast we were again engaged by heavy flak, flying through smoke puffs. The only manoeuvre possible was on fore and aft control, which I applied, and, in doing so, broke away the perpendicular piece of main plane. This gave me about 10 per cent aileron control. As engines were Ok, I decided to make for WOODBRIDGE and gave the navigator the necessary instructions. We kept about 25 miles from enemy coast in case of emergency when we would have had to make an emergency landing. I then ordered a bombing check, but found that 4 TI's and 2 X 1,000 MC bombs were still hung up. I ordered, too, more bombing checks, but with same results. I contemplated sending engineer back to release manually, but the handling of aircraft was such that prolonged flying with bomb doors open caused too much loss of height, and so considered that it was better not to release manually. Furthermore I required the engineer at my side. When 45 miles from enemy coast, I ordered Wireless Operator to transmit emergency call, stating position, GEE course, speed and height. Also later contacted base to tell them I was landing at WOODBRIDGE. The engineer suggested using petrol from port tanks, thus lightening the load on damaged side, which I substantiated and this resulted in slightly better flying conditions. At 0307 hrs we made land fall at English coast heading directly for WOODBRIDGE and switched on TR 1196 Channel D. Darky frequency. I lost height to 1,500 ft, transmitting all the time, but failed to receive a reply because aerial shot away, but received a green from A.P.C. Previously I had tested the undercarriage at 13,000 ft and found it serviceable, but the stalling speed with the undercarriage down was 140 knots. I therefore made my approach 1,500 ft 2 miles from aerodrome, using plenty of motor, air speed 150 knots. I came into the Green of the glide path indicator 400 yards from runway, brought my speed back to 145 and touched down approx three quarters down runway on emergency flare path at 140 knots. I felt the port side drop which indicated I had a flat port tyre and immediately applied right rudder. Because of stalling speed I could not lift the left wing except by right rudder and after a few hundred yards, the Oleo leg collapsed and the port wing dug into the ground, swinging me over to the starboard Oleo leg which also collapsed, and we skidded off runway in a belly position with a swing approx 30 deg. to port, full right rudder still applied. We continued for approx 150 yards and finished up with a loop to port 180 degs and stopped. At 2,000 ft I had ordered crash position for crew, except engineer, so nobody was hurt and as soon as aircraft stopped I ordered the engineer "Everything off – undertake evacuation". I climbed through the side window, engineer through Pilot's hatch and crew through mid upper hatch. The ambulance and crash party were stopped 20 yards in front and I ran over to them and assured myself that their equipment was in immmediate readiness. I then went back to aircraft, counted crew, found all unhurt, and ordered them to get away from the aircraft. The success of the mission and prolonged difficult return was greatly assisted by excellent crew co-operation, particularly by navigator and engineer.'*

S/L Slade was awarded an immediate D.S.O. for what was a superb combination of high courage, leadership and skilled airmanship. He died back home in his native Australia in 1969.

There was a daylight raid on July 30th in the area of Villers Bocage, to aid the advancing armies, and the month ended with two pairs of Master Bombers and Deputy Master Bombers operating against two separate targets. S/L Ison, D.F.C., and F/L Doyle led a raid on Le Havre (one of several to come), while

F/L A. W. G. Cochrane, D.F.C., was the Master Bomber and S/L G. C. Hemmings was Deputy in a raid on Foret-du-Croc.

July had been a month in which the Pathfinders and the entire command had excelled themselves. The Upwood Squadron 156 had extended themselves in an amazing way, with groups of aircraft raiding three separate targets in one day and night. The ground crews in particular worked magnificently, often getting the same few aircraft ready for two raids in a twenty-four hour period. This month the squadron had broken its own record with a total of 271 operational sorties, with one aircraft missing. It felt good to be a Pathfinder member of aircrew on 156 Squadron in July 1944.

V-Weapons and German Targets

The first few days of August saw an increase in the attacks on the V-Weapon sites. On the first there were two flying bomb sites to attack and 156 provided the Master Bomber and Deputy for each, F/L Doyle and S/L Griffin D.F.C., for Prouville, and F/L 't Hart, D.F.C. and F/L Wilson for Coulon Villers, though, on account of ten-tenths cloud, this last raid was abortive. Ten aircraft from Upwood went to the Bois de Cassan supply site on August 3rd, while four attacked the flying-bomb stores at Trossy-St-Maxim on the 4th, and eight attacked an oil-storage depot at Pauillac. It was on the raid on Trossy-St-Maxim that a posthumous V.C. was awarded to S/L I. W. Bazalgette of 635 Pathfinder Squadron from Downham Market. The next day eight Lancasters from Upwood attacked the Foret de Nieppe storage sites for the flying bomb launchers, while another six raided Coulon Villers. The next day, by contrast, on August 6th, six Upwood aircraft attacked the Hazebrouck marshalling yards. General Eisenhower had requested attacks on flying bomb sites, marshalling yards and, whenever they lay in the path of the advancing allies, troop concentrations. The supreme command was also reaching out to bleed away Hitler's oil, which was, of course, his life blood. On the 7th a tragic accident occurred which saddened the entire squadron. Returning from the night's operation, a visit to the Normandy battle area, a Mosquito crashed into one of the married quarters at Upwood where aircrew were sleeping. Two sleeping aircrew members were killed, F/S L. A. Rookes (a bomb aimer) and F/S Winlow (a navigator). The two Mosquito aircrew were also killed. The next day the bodies of the two 156 aircrew members were sent home for burial.

The Fort d'Englos storage site for the flying bombs was raided in a night operation on August 9th, and the Somain marshalling yards on the 11th. Over Russelsheim on the night of the next day, the 12th, the incredible run of luck the squadron had been having, before that ghastly accident on August 7th, was broken once again. Two Lancasters out of Upwood's contribution of sixteen did not come back. Both were captained by experienced pilots who had each done a recent trip as Deputy Master Bomber, F/L J. N. McDonald, D.F.M., and S/L

G. C. Hemmings, D.F.C. Their target over Russelsheim had been the Opel factory, and their loss to the squadron was keenly felt, at a time when the crews, who had lived from the early months of the year to this point, were thinking that they just might live forever. On the day of that night raid a distinguished and experienced operational pilot, W/C D. B. Falconer, D.F.C., A.F.C., was posted to Upwood and 156 Squadron from 571 Squadron, based at Oakington, one of the Mosquito squadrons, which made up the celebrated Light Night Striking Force. He was destined, before the year was out, to become 156 Squadron's C.O. and to be lost over Cologne on the last day but one of 1944.

On August 14th fifteen aircraft took off from Upwood to bomb an area near Falaise where there were German troop dispositions which were facing the third Canadian division. Due to a mistake over yellow identification flares some of the allied troops were bombed. The Master Bomber tried his best to stop crews from bombing in this area, but not before thirteen Canadians were killed and fifty-three were wounded. When the bombs began to fall on our own troops, their signals officer immediately let off the colours of the day, as they had been taught to do when aircraft of the Tactical Air Force were overhead and were bombing dangerously near. Bomber Command and the Pathfinders had been told nothing about this arrangement, however, and the yellow smoke let off by the ground troops unhappily compared with (and looked uncommonly like) the yellow 'daylight' T.Is dropped as the markers on the aiming point by the Pathfinders. It was an unhappy and unfortunate blunder, caused, as all these things are caused, by the rapid dispositions and reactions required in the stress of war; but it was not Bomber Command's fault, and not the fault of the Pathfinders.

The next day (August 15th) saw eleven aircraft take off from Upwood to bomb German night fighter airfields, two proceeding to Volkel and attacking it, while the rest attacked Eindhoven, home to many of the night fighters who had wreaked such havoc in the bomber stream earlier in the year. The raid, with all its complications, diversions, and individual waves and flights, was a 'maximum effort' on the part of 1,004 aircraft, out of which three Lancasters were lost, none from 156. The next night it was back to Germany, with two raids on Kiel and Stettin respectively. The Lancasters taking part in the Stettin attack numbered 461, and five were lost. Five were also lost from the force of 346 which set out that night to bomb Kiel, although none of these were from Upwood.

An interesting night occurred two days after the Kiel raid, when, on August 18th the squadron was split, some to attack Bremen, others to pound the last (though the crews did not know it) in the series of French targets, Connantre, a railway station with railway yards seventy miles east of Paris. This was the end of the prolonged and almost continuous series of raids on Belgian and French railway targets. On this target S/L Attwater, D.F.C. was Master Bomber; while F/L Cochrane was Deputy Master Bomber. For the second time in the month the Opel motor factory at Russelsheim was attacked. The sixteen Upwood aircraft all attacked and returned safely on the night of August 25th, which must have been a relief to squadron aircrew, who remembered how a fortnight before they had lost two crews, whose captains had acted as Deputy Master Bombers, over this target. And yet the next night (August 26th) on a raid to Kiel F/L Etchells went missing, one of the seventeen Lancasters missing that night.

The crew captained by F/L Etchells were attacked by a JU88 over the target. During the attack hits from return fire were observed on the German fighter, and it was shot down. With one engine on fire, two feathered and in a severely damaged condition, the Lancaster ditched in the North Sea on the return, and the crew clambered into their dinghy. The next day, a Sunday, a friendly aircraft sighted the crew drifting in the sea and an inflatable lifeboat was dropped to reach them. This they could not reach, however, and the next day another aircraft dropped a Lindholme dinghy. Heroic efforts were made to reach this lifeboat, with the rear gunner swimming off alone to get to it, and still not being able to reach it. Nevertheless, at last they came within reach of the boat, and occupied it. The very next day (Monday) their second day on the deep, there were such rough seas that the lifeboat was almost swamped. At a point of absolute desperation when the boat was sinking fast, and the crew could not bale out the water fast enough, a Danish fishing boat was seen on the horizon. It came near, and took them aboard. The four Danish fishermen were not at all keen on taking them back to England, although a chaperoning Hudson dropped instructions in a cannister to them instructing them to sail for England. On Tuesday at 1700 hours an air-sea recue launch took them on board, and the launch and the Danish fishing boat arrived at Grimsby. There was rejoicing at Upwood when the news came through. F/L Etchells became known henceforth as 'Dinghy' Etchells.

Meanwhile, though it was back to Germany with oil and transport targets, the flying bomb campaign still continued. A day after F/L Etchells went missing there was a daylight raid on Mimoyecques. No Upwood aircraft failed to get back (indeed the entire Command effort was without loss) but P/O Freeman had to land his aircraft on three engines at Manston, after it had been riddled by flak, some of which had entered the nose of the Lancaster and wounded the bomb aimer. S/Ls Attwood and Cochrane led this raid as Master and Deputy. A raid to Stettin proceeded the next night with none missing out of sixteen dispatched. The crews were in good heart as the news that F/L Etchells and his crew had come ashore at Grimsby had reached them during the day. The last day of August saw daylight operations on two targets, with the C.O., W/C Bingham-Hall, acting as Master Bomber and F/L Doyle as Deputy against a V-2 rocket store at Limbres, while S/Ls Attwater and Cochrane, the 'old firm', played the same role against another V-2 storage site at St. Riquier. The next day, September 1st, S/L Attwater D.F.C. and his crew were screened, with a total of 424 operations between them. Although the squadron was sorry to lose the crew, their screening gave immense encouragement. There actually was, for some, for an increasing number, a life after Pathfinders.

Le Havre and French Targets

On September 3rd six airfields in southern Holland were raided. Upwood sent nine aircraft to Eindhoven on this daylight operation, in a classic controlled visual attack. The next few operations were to Le Havre, where the German garrison was under siege. On September 5th, 6th, 7th, 8th, 9th and 10th the bomber force went out to raid the German troop dispositions around Le Havre. These troops had been bypassed by the allies in their advance. Upwood provided the Master and Deputy Master Bombers on all these raids. These were on the 5th the C.O. and S/L Ison, on the 6th S/Ls Ison and Cochrane, and on the 8th S/Ls Ison and Cochrane. On the 9th, when W/C Bingham-Hall, the C.O. was again the Master Bomber, five Lancasters sent to Le Havre had to abort the mission and return to Upwood with their bombs. Over the target there were thunderstorms and ten tenths cloud. The Squadron C.O. roared over Le Havre at 300 feet, below the thunderclouds. Just earlier than this he had sent out the broadcast code 'Apple Pie' to abandon the operation. A flurry of light flak peppered W/C Bingham-Hall's aircraft. The Lancaster seemed to have as many holes as a colander, and black smoke was seen to pour out from the starboard outer engine. The mid-upper gunner 'Bill' Shepherd hosepiped the gun emplacements, and the Lancaster staggered back to England, literally, at times, skimming the waves. Fortunately the starboard outer engine had stopped smoking, when it was feathered. A crash landing later occurred at Upwood, still with the bombs on board. When these bombs, at the dispersal, had been removed by the groundcrew, and were already on the trailer and about to be towed away, they exploded, with a roar that could be heard for miles around, and which rattled the windows in Upwood, Ramsey, Warboys and beyond.

The consequences were grievous and horrific. Seven airmen were killed, of whom four had simply disappeared, and were classified as 'Missing, believed killed'. Standing at another dispersal and looking across, Taff Jones saw the whole thing. Some of his friends died in that explosion, among them Cpl. Gill, Cpl. Mole, L.A.C. Graham, L.A.C. Jones and AC1 Ellis. His girlfriend, Norah Shephard (now his wife), working in the N.A.A.F.I. back in R.A.F. Warboys, was convinced that Taff was one of the casualties. It was only much later that she could obtain reassurance; but the entire airfield community was stunned, and the villages surrounding, where the men were known, and the homes where they had entry. Death was not a faraway thing on an operational station. You hardly ever saw death on an airfield, however, even though dead and dying aircrew were occasionally brought back in a crippled Lancaster. The accident brought home what the authorities knew all along, that the casualty rate among the armourers was second only to that of aircrew.

In this same explosion the flight engineer, Norman Piercy, in the C.O's crew had his leg blown off, and every Lancaster in 'B' flight was, in some way, damaged in the blast. Three days later, on September 12th, out on 'B' flight dispersal a memorial service was held for the airmen who had lost their lives in that explosion, and for whom no burial was possible. And yet, a day after the explosion, on the morning of the 10th, the squadron was operational again, and six Lancasters raided Le Havre.

Germany was not being neglected during this extremely volatile period. A large raid to Emden took place on the 6th, the same day as the second in the series of Le Havre raids, and some Lancasters from 156 joined in this. On the Emden raid only one Lancaster was lost. It was not from Upwood, but from Oakington, and was the aircraft of the Deputy Master Bomber, F/L Granville Wilson, D.S.O., D.F.C., D.F.M, a twenty-three year old Northern Irishman of great courage and experience. A flak shell struck his Lancaster as he orbited the target, killing him instantly, together with his navigator and bomb aimer. The other five crew members baled out.

Oil Targets

Synthetic oil plants, so necessary to Germany's continuation of the war, now that natural oil fields had virtually been bombed out of existence, were attacked increasingly during this period. In his many arguments and frequent correspondence with Sir Charles Portal and his superiors in the Air Ministry, Sir Arthur Harris would argue that these were 'panacea targets', and that it was the bombing of entire cities that would shorten the war. For all that, he attacked the oil targets he was given: on September 10th thirteen Upwood aircraft went on a daylight raid to Gelsenkirchen, losing one experienced crew captained by S/L A. W. Raw. The target was very well defended (synthetic oil was the Reich's only hope at this time) and ten aircraft landed at Upwood damaged by flak. On the next day, the day that the German garrison at Le Havre at last surrendered, and the day on which the memorial service for the victims of the airfield explosion was held, five aircraft visited another oil target, Scholven, in daylight, while sixteen took off on a night raid to Frankfurt. There were no casualties on either of these raids, and the news that 'Dinghy' Etchells had been awarded the D.S.O. cheered the squadron. The next day, September 13th, the Nordstern oil plant at Gelsenkirchen was raided again, while, to add variety and in complete contrast, on the next day an ammunition dump, possibly a V-2 store, at Wassenar, near the Hague, was blown up by a small force of bombers, including five from Upwood. S/L Cochrane and F/L Doyle were Master and Deputy Master Bomber. A highly concentrated night raid, in the old style, took place on September 15th on Kiel, a target of unhappy memory for 156, although all sixteen aircraft came back to Upwood that night.

To have in your log book an oil target, a raid on a V-2 store, an area attack on a German city, and a raid in support of ground troop movements is part of the character of this period of 1944 for Pathfinders, and for 156 Squadron. On the night of September 16th Bomber Command operations took place in support of the drops at Arnhem and Nijmegen which took place the next morning. Six Lancasters of 156 bombed a flak site at Moerdijk Bridge. On the 15th W/C R. J. Burrough, the 'A' flight commander, was posted from the squadron to command 128 Squadron, newly re-formed at Wyton, as part of the Pathfinder Light Night Striking Force. The Mosquitoes of this squadron were to take part in a very special operation on New Year's Day, 1945, the 'skip' bombing of the Coblenz railway tunnels, as part of the programme of continuous disruption of transport.

Coming in advance of the allied armies to bomb Boulogne on September 17th, S/L Cochrane acted as Master Bomber, while the C.O. was Deputy Master Bomber. Again, in support of operation *Market Garden*, the Arnhem and Nijmegen drops, the flak positions around Flushing were attacked that same day with F/Ls Doyle and Clayton as Master Bomber and Deputy. The next day F/L Clayton was Master Bomber and F/O Lewis Deputy for a raid on the Domburg heavy coastal battery, although ten tenths cloud caused the mission to be aborted. S/L Ison was Master Bomber in an attack on the 20th on German positions around Calais, there was a successful daylight raid on the docks and factories of Neuss on the 23rd, while on the 24th F/L Ken Doyle, D.F.C. and his crew, acting as a 'Long Stop' for another raid on Calais, failed to return, the only aircraft involved in this raid from Upwood. The duty of the 'Long Stop' was to cancel any marking that was wild, or to put limits on the bombing by dropping yellow T.Is, a measure extremely necessary where the lives of allied troops and French civilians were in danger. Although the skymarkers were dropped by Oboe Mosquitoes, some aircraft had to dive down below the cloud to bomb visually. That was when the light flak got Ken Doyle, and six other Lancasters, and one Halifax. The defences had a field day. A Master Bomber from another squadron was badly riddled with flak. He handed over to his Deputy who suffered the same fate, and handed over to a Backer-Up, who went on controlling the attack even though the starboard inner engine had to be feathered, and the port inner engine was damaged. F/L Ken Doyle and his crew was one of the squadron's most grievous losses. He had been with 156 since the dark days of the Battle of Berlin. In a raid on that city on February 15th, his rear gunner, Sgt. Geoff. Smith, had won a C.G.M., after being so severely wounded that he had to have a leg amputated. Ken Doyle's flight engineer from those earlier days of his first tour, Syd Richardson, writes with affection of his skipper in some notes in *The 156 Register*. F/L Doyle, that gallant Australian, was well into his second tour with 156 Squadron when he was killed. He was a notable member of those 'mighty men of valour' (to use a biblical phrase) who made up 156 Squadron's select band of Master Bombers and Deputy Master Bombers.

The next day, September 25th, it was back to Calais, with six aircraft from Upwood taking part, among them the C.O. as Master Bomber, and W/C Falconer as his Deputy. Two more attacks on Calais followed that month, one on the 27th (W/C Falconer as Master Bomber and F/O G. Lewis as Deputy), and one on the 28th (with F/Ls Clayton and Wilson as Master Bombers and with F/L M. W. Kitson and F/O G. Lewis as Deputies). The synthetic oil plants at Bottrop also received attention on September 27th and on September 30th. As a part of the campaign against the German defensive positions at Calais, six Upwood aircraft joined in an attack on nearby Cap Gris Nez on September 26th. Calais (another 'Le Havre'), after these attacks in late September, finally capitulated. Without Bomber Command, and without precision Pathfinder marking, it is doubtful whether the French channel ports could have been cleared as early as this.

'Le Havres', beleagured German garrisons were showing up with regular frequency at this time. From October 3rd until 30th a series of raids, Pathfinder led, were made on the sea walls of Walcheren, with the clear intentions of flooding the island, submerging the gun batteries and denying the enemy that grip they had on the approaches to Antwerp. S/L Cochrane D.F.C., and F/L P. F. Clayton, D.F.C. played their parts as Master and Deputy. On the last Walcheren attack, on October 29th, there was a pair of Master Bombers (S/L Cochrane and F/L Clayton) and a pair of Deputies (F/L Harris and F/L Lewis). Meanwhile Saarbrucken (remember how it was last raided in the early Pathfinder days in September 1942) was visited on the night of October 5/6th, Dortmund on 6/7th, Kleve on a daylight raid on October 7th, Bochum on 9/10th, and an important oil plant at Wanne-Eickel on October 12th. Duisburg received its heaviest pounding of the war on October 14th. Upwood provided fifteen aircraft for the day attack and fifteen for a night raid. W/C Ison and F/L Wilson acted as Master Bomber and Deputy for the daylight raid. The Americans also sent in a wave of bombers during the day. Out of the 1,013 R.A.F. aircraft thirteen Lancasters and one Halifax were lost. The night raid consisted of 1,005 bombers which attacked Duisburg again in two different waves two hours apart. From these two waves five Lancasters and two Halifaxes were lost, though none from 156. On October 15th Wilhelmshaven was raided, while Stuttgart was bombed on the 19th. There were also two raids on Essen, one on October 21st, a night raid, while on October 25th a 'daylight' took place in which W/C Falconer, D.F.C., A.F.C., was Master Bomber and F/L Clayton D.F.C. was Deputy Master Bomber. Skymarkers were used, and the target, obscured by nine or ten tenths cloud, was bombed on these skymarkers. This period of the war, in terms of the emphasis on choice of targets, whenever German towns were concerned, was called the Second Battle of the Ruhr. During this month of October the C.O. was promoted to the acting rank of Group Captain, while S/L R. F. Griffin, D.F.C. and S/L L. A. Dwen, two outstanding pilots who had many operations to their credit, were on October 22nd awarded immediate

D.S.Os. Furthermore, when the analysis for the past three months of Blind Bombing performance was made, 156 Squadron was found to head the Pathfinder Force.

November 1944 opened with a raid, through ten tenths cloud, on Oberhausen. On the 2nd S/L Cochrane nearly came to grief on take-off for Dusseldorf, in a celebrated incident which has been recounted in several publications. S/L Cochrane the New Zealander, known variously as 'Cocky' or 'Kiwi Cochrane', who had attacked a number of times as Master Bomber, was taking off, with a replacement flight engineer. This new member did not know that it was Cocky's habit to talk to his Lancaster when it was straining to lift off the ground, and take off. Sometimes he used to chasten the aircraft with his tongue just before it got airborne. This he did, saying, 'Up, you bastard, up, you bastard.' The new flight engineer thought these directions were for him, and immediately lifted the undercarriage. The Lancaster then slid across the runway with a 4,000lb 'cookie' at about 40 miles an hour. The bomb aimer, P/O Dee, leapt out, as did other crew members, notwithstanding the speed of the aircraft. By some quirk P/O Dee, another New Zealander, was seen rolling like a ball approaching the aircraft he had left at such speed from an opposite direction! This could have been utterly disastrous for all concerned. Why the 'cookie' did not explode is nothing short of miraculous.

Among the new arrivals at this time was F/L J. B. Nicholls and crew from Warboys and the N.T.U. F/L Nicholls was a Welsh rugby international. Bochum and Gelsenkirchen were both visited early in the month. A skilled Canadian navigator F/L Chislett was promoted to Acting Squadron Leader. He flew with F/L Jack Cuthill, just before the latter was screened, and promoted to Squadron Leader. From the 6th to the 16th there was a stand down, while on November 16th eleven Upwood aircraft took part in a massive attack on Duren, to prepare the way for an American advance. Nearly 3,000 British and U.S. aircraft (including fighters) took part in this thunderous bombardment. Excellent marking was put down, and the Long Stop, W/C Falconer, did not need to drop his yellow T.Is, because the bombing was so accurate. When the Lancasters came back to Upwood, however, the weather had closed in, and visibility was almost nil. Only four out of the eleven landed at Upwood, while the rest were diverted. The C.O. and S/L Clayton, D.F.C.(he had recently been promoted) were Marker and Deputy on a raid on Munster on November 18th. An unusual all Pathfinder raid took place on the night of 20/21st November. Koblenz was the target, and doubtless the aiming-points were road and rail bridges over the Rhine and Mosel, although there are no details about the raid's exact purpose. Eight Blind Marker aircraft from Upwood assisted in this, bombing from 15,000 feet by H2S. On the night of the 21/22nd November there were three targets: six aircraft from the squadron attacked Aschaffenburg, and the local railway yards and vital rail network, six more attacked Sterkrade, and the synthetic oil factory which had been a target visited previously on a number of occasions, and three Lancasters attacked Worms. This is an illustration of the versatility of command and control, and the ability of administration, groundcrew, and aircrew to take in different targets in a limited time both in terms of preparation, and execution. There were no losses to the squadron from this hectic day. That same day, the day before the night the three targets were attacked, G/C Bingham-Hall D.S.O., D.F.C. ceased to be Squadron C.O. on being posted to Oakington as Station Commander. Bill Davies, second navigator, or set operator in F/O K. T. Wallace's crew, who had only just arrived on the squadron, speaks of the tears rolling down G/C Bingham-Hall's cheeks on his being presented with a silver cigarette case by the aircrew of 156 one morning before his departure. W/C Falconer, D.F.C., A.F. C. was appointed to succeed him.

Before the end of the month Freiburg, Essen and Duisburg were bombed. The night raid on Freiburg on November 27th, with the experienced pair W/C Ison and S/L Clayton controlling the bombing, was an extremely effective attack. The main railway station, marshalling yards and the main barracks in the town were completely destroyed. One Lancaster, from another squadron, was lost. Neuss was raided on the same night, with two Upwood Lancasters joining in as Supporters. S/L Cochrane D.F.C. was awarded during this month, in recognition of a brilliant operational career with the squadron, an immediate D.S.O. The next month another experienced Master Bomber W/C T. E. Ison, D.F.C. was accorded the same honour.

December saw more German towns attacked, Karlsruhe on the night of the 4/5th, Soest on the 5/6th (an intense and concentrated attack in which the marshalling yards 'could be distinguished briefly in the flashes of bomb bursts', as the *Operations Record Book* remarks), Osnabruck on the 6/7th, and Essen on the 12/13th, the last night attack on Essen by Bomber Command. On December 14th a note appeared in the Bomber Command Summary saying that the raid on Freiburg was assessed by the neutral press as one of the most outstanding in the war. That was the raid in which W/C Ison was Master Bomber. On December 6th Upwood had received a new Station Commander. G/C J. L. Airey, D.F.C. was succeeded by G/C 'Paddy' Menaul, D.F.C., A.F.C., whose early operational career had been with XV Squadron, flying from various locations in the fens.

On December 17th two Lancasters were lost on a raid on Ulm. One of the missing aircraft was that of F/L L. N. B. Cann, D.F.C. of 156 Squadron.

Bad weather kept the crews from operating for three days. When the fog had thinned out a little eleven Lancasters from Upwood took off to attack Bonn, and, once again, as in the case of other attacks, railway yards and networks were the target. This was an attack carried out in ten-tenths cloud under extremely difficult conditions, and was designed to assist allied soldiers who were being pushed back during the recent German Ardennes offensive, Hitler's 'last gamble'. The same urgency underlay the daylight operations on December

24th, a massive attack on some major German airfields. Supplies must, at all costs, be prevented from reaching the Ardennes front. Only two Upwood aircraft took off, that of S/L Cochrane and that of F/L G. Lewis who were Master Bomber and Deputy Master Bomber of the attack on the airfield at Dusseldorf. Extreme weather conditions caused both aircraft to divert to Graveley on their return. The crews of these two aircraft were back that evening to take part in a party and dance held in the Station N.A.A.F.I. given by the aircrew to the ground crew on the station. The next day, Christmas Day, saw the traditional Airmen's Christmas Dinner, with officers and senior N.C.Os acting as waiters. The Station N.A.A.F.I. that evening was the venue for an All Ranks Cabaret Dance.

After three days respite, enforced by fog and bad weather, the marshalling yards at Opladen were bombed in an early morning attack on the 28th, with ten Lancasters from Upwood taking part. A 'daylight' took place the next day (December 29th) on Koblenz and the railway yards which constituted one of the main communications centres feeding the Ardennes battle front. The defence was resolute and F/O W. H. Cornelius was wounded by a flak splinter which penetrated his left heel. His engineer also came back wounded. And so was set in motion the chain of events which resulted the next day, December 30th, in the new C.O., W/C Donald Falconer, taking the crew of F/O Cornelius, with the Squadron Engineer Leader F/L W. N. Bingham substituting for the engineer wounded the previous day on a trip to the Kalk railway yards in Cologne. The C.O. and his crew failed to return from this night raid, the only Lancaster missing (although one Halifax also failed to return). W/C Falconer, D.F.C., A.F.C., that distinguished Master Bomber, had been C.O. for just over five weeks. He had a long career in Bomber Command, having won his D.F.C. during a tour on Hampdens early in the war. The next day W/C Ison, D.S.O., D.F.C., who was then the 'B' flight commander took over temporary command of the squadron, although he was soon to be confirmed in permanent command, and on the last day of that momentous year, 1944, there took place a night raid on the railway yards at Osterfeld, which, for all the aircraft taking part, including eight from Upwood, quite literally, saw in the New Year.

Finale

January 1945 began with raids on a series of German towns in all of which 156 Squadron and the Pathfinders took a leading part. Dortmund on the night of January 1/2nd (when a benzol plant was attacked), Nuremberg on the next night, 2/3rd, the German garrison at Royan, away from the German cities, in the early hours of the morning of January 5th, a large attack on Hannover on the 5/6th and an attack upon vital railway junctions at Hanau on the 6/7th. Munich was visited on the next night (7/8th), the last major raid on the city for the rest of the war, the synthetic oil plant at Leuna on the night of the 14/15th, and Gelsenkirchen, the most frequently visited of the oil targets, on 22/23rd January (shared with a raid on a benzol plant in Duisburg). It is undoubtedly true that Sir Arthur Harris gave as much attention to the oil targets as to area attacks even though a controversial correspondence between himself and Sir Charles Portal suggests otherwise, but with the vast operational strength, at this period in Bomber Command, it was possible for the C. in C. both to pursue the oil and communications plan, in his selection of targets, and to attack those cities which were important centres of support for the Reich war machine, some of them not so well damaged as others. That fatal early 1944 target, Magdeburg, was attacked on the night of 16/17th January, and, though there were no Upwood casualties, seventeen Halifaxes were lost, one of the largest casualty figures of this period. Duisburg on January 22/23rd was raided, another 'old friend', which had received a number of raids in the past two months, everyone declaring that it had been irrevocably destroyed. On January 28/29th, in a raid on Stuttgart, split into two waves, with an interval of three hours between each one, one of the Upwood Lancasters failed to return, that of F/L J. H. Freeman. He and his crew were to be the only casualties of this month. This was, of course, no special comfort to their families and loved ones. But the loss of these last few aircraft and crews was regarded as being specially tragic, now that the end for which all had fought and died was in sight.

On the first night of the new month (February 1/2nd) Mainz, not visited since early Pathfinder days in 1942, was the target. Wiesbaden, Bomber Command's one and only large raid, was attacked the next night, with the benzol plant at Bottrop furnishing a target the next night (February 3/4th). Oil targets were, in the experience of aircrew, very well defended at this time. Oil plants were the lifeblood of the dying Reich, and to bomb them was to drain it away. There was good marking and a concentrated pattern, but aircraft were getting coned in the many searchlights, just like the Essen of early 1943, and night fighters were active. Two aircraft, of the nine that had set out from Upwood that night 'to drain the oil of Bottrop' (*Operations Record Book* entry for February 3rd, 1945) failed to return, those captained by F/L M. Spinley, D.F.M. and by F/L J. G. Evans. So fast was the pace of the allied advance that news of the first of these missing aircraft reached the squadron two days later. F/L Spinley's Lancaster disintegrated in mid-air near Hechtel in Belgium. The news was that only the rear gunner had survived. Later it was discovered that there were other survivors. The pilot, however, who had a D.F.M., an experienced operational captain from New Zealand, had been killed instantly.

A raid on enemy troop concentrations at Goch, lying just ahead of the British XXX Corps, and shortly to be engaged in the opening round of what was called the Battle of the Reichswald, took place on February 7th. S/L Cochrane was Master Bomber and F/L Harris his Deputy, and there was good marking throughout. When the bombing by the main force began to suffer slightly, due to the rising smoke, the Master Bomber called off the attack. A week later a signal was received from the General Officer Commanding the Canadian Army via H.Q. Bomber Command expressing appreciation of the support the bombers had given to the advancing allies. The Master and Deputy had been supplied by 156 and the *Operations Record Book* records this congratulation and underlines the contribution made by the pair who controlled the raid. Severe damage was done also to a very important synthetic oil plant at Politz by a raid taking place on February 8th. Once again 156 provided Master Bomber, S/L J. A. Wilson, and Deputy Master Bomber, F/L G. L ewis, D.F.C. Of the fourteen aircraft from Upwood detailed for that raid, two could not proceed on account of technical failure.

A skilled pilot from the P.N.T.U. at Warboys was posted to Upwood on February 12th to take over the crew of F/L Jack Cuthill, D.F.C. This was S/L Peter Hague who had been instructing at the Pathfinder N.T.U. at Warboys, having gone there from 576 Squadron. Jack Cuthill had been 'screened', together with the two gunners who had been with him since the early days at the O.T.U. at Finningley, W/O Ron Smith, the rear gunner (whose book *Rear Gunner Pathfinders* is a vivid and important contribution to any understanding of these times), and W/O Dougie Aspinall, the mid-upper gunner. Soon Jack Cuthill was promoted to Squadron Leader and awarded a well deserved D.S.O. S/L J. Cuthill, D.S.O., D.F.C. left the squadron to serve as an instructor for the remainder of the war.

On the night of February 13th there were two targets for the Upwood aircraft. Seven Lancasters attacked the oil plant at Bohlen near Leipzig, while nine joined in the attack made on Dresden by 796 Lancasters and nine Mosquitoes. The first wave attack on Dresden was made entirely by 5 Group aircraft, while the next one, three hours afterwards, was carried out by aircraft of 1, 3, 6 and 8 Groups. Crews of 156 who came in on this second wave reported that 'extensive fires were burning from a previous wave', and that 'Several explosions were reported, and the town was burning from end to end'. Because of the loss of life sustained during this attack, which exceeded the number of those who died in the Hamburg firestorm of July 1943, this raid, and the choice of Dresden as a target, has been laid at the door of the C. in C. Bomber Command, Sir Arthur Harris by a post-war generation of writers and commentators. It must be said that the choice of Dresden as a target (and other cities in the east like Leipzig and Chemnitz) was part of a deliberate set of plans code-named *Operation Thunderclap*, initiated and approved by the Air Ministry. The aim was to dislocate these cities to such an extent that morale in them would be completely broken down, and so that, at the point of the Russian advance, it would be totally impossible to pour reinforcements from the west to face this eastern threat. So Sir Arthur Harris did as the Air Ministry requested, with the Prime Minister's active encouragement. Although the Prime Minister sought to distance himself from this raid afterwards, the Official History emphasises that Mr Winston Churchill took a hand in it. The raid to Chemnitz on the next night, on February 14/15th, was not different in its execution and implementation from the Dresden raid of the night before. It was the weather, and the ten tenths cloud, which saved Chemnitz. Once again, it was a two wave attack, with nine Upwood Lancasters taking part in the first wave, and seven joining in the second. There was a resort to skymarkers, *Wanganui* flares, and, although much damage was done, many bombs fell in open country. Crews of 156 saw five aircraft shot down on this raid, although, like the night before, there were no casualties from the squadron. Six Lancasters from the Command as a whole were lost on the Dresden raid (with two additional aircraft crashing in France, and one in England), while the raid to Chemnitz cost the Command eight Lancasters and five Halifaxes. S/L Cochrane was the Master Bomber on a daylight raid on Wesel on February 17th. Not even a glow was seen when the T.Is went down and disappeared into cloud. Diving down from 15,000 to 3,000 feet the Master Bomber ordered the mission aborted, after only eight Halifaxes had bombed.

There were still casualties at a time when the urgent priority was to shorten the war and avoid further suffering, in the air and on the ground by whatever means. In a 5 Group only raid on Bohlen on the night of February 19/20th the Master Bomber, W/C E. A. Benjamin, D.F.C. and Bar, was shot down over the target. On the next night 8 Group and 156 Squadron were out over two targets, the Reisholz district of Dusseldorf, where there was an oil refinery, and Dortmund, a bottleneck for the Ruhr traffic. Only two out of sixteen aircraft dispatched from Upwood attacked the first target, and F/L A. D. Pelly and his crew failed to return. A large attack on Worms, the only large attack of the war, occurred the next night. A secondary target was bombed by one of the Upwood crews, F/L Grant, as a fire in one of his engines made him twenty minutes late for the primary. The attack on Pforzheim on February 23/24th saw the last V.C. of the war won by a Bomber Command man. It was one of the Pathfinders who won it, Captain Edwin Swales, the Master Bomber, and a South African serving with 582 Squadron at Little Staughton. Despite being attacked frequently over the target Captain Swales continued to direct the bombing. Setting out on the return with a badly damaged Lancaster he ordered the crew to bale out, despite being unable to do so himself. Ten Upwood aircraft took part, and returning crews reported seeing the flames from 100 miles away. One pilot and crew showed exemplary 'press on' spirit. F/O W. F. Keeler had to feather one of his engines shortly after take-off. Despite this grave handicap, he pressed on, arrived at the target on time, making the complete flight in six and a half hours. A 'daylight' the next day on a synthetic oil plant in Kamen, involving five 156 aircraft, was carried out in conditions of ten tenths cloud, the tops of which reached up to 9,000 feet. At the end of a most hectic and varied month, S/L Cochrane was awarded a second Bar to his D.F.C. With a D.S.O. and two Bars to his D.F.C., Kiwi Cockrane, Cocky to his friends, was becoming the squadron's most celebrated Master Bomber.

Five days after his eventful trip to Pforzheim, F/O Keeler was tested to the limit yet again. Out of the eleven aircraft that set out from Upwood on March 1st, for a daylight attack on Mannheim, one returned early, the rest had to orbit the target until the main force, very much behind time, arrived, and yet again the engine in one of these aircraft, F/O Keeler's, cut out. This time he was fifty minutes away from the target, and yet, in typical fashion, he pressed on, was in time over the target, and, once more, arrived back at base on three engines. Back at interrogation F/O Keeler reported that he believed that pieces of an exploding aircraft hit his own Lancaster, causing the engine failure. Two hours away from the target an engine failed in the Lancaster flown by F/O Boggiano. Nevertheless, he too pressed on, bombed late, and landed at Upwood one hour and twenty minutes after the others had come back. Spitfires picked him up as he was coming home, struggling behind all the rest, and escorted him to safety. Both F/O Keeler and F/O Boggiano received immediate D.F.Cs.

After this daylight raid of varied fortunes for Upwood aircraft, a trouble-free daylight trip to Cologne ensued on the next day. Cologne, these days, was a city protecting the western line of the Reich, with the Americans about to enter it. It had many troops and tanks bolstering its fortress potential. This punishing raid on Cologne with S/L Clayton, D.S.O., D.F.C. as Master Bomber and F/L W. J. Cleland, D.F.C., the popular 'Ginger' Cleland, as Deputy, was the last of the war, and four days later the Americans arrived in the city. On the night of March 5/6th it was the turn of Chemnitz again, one of the classic *Operation Thunderclap* targets. The Pathfinders marked well and the raid advanced well. The *Operations Record Book* of 156 ventures to hope that this attack 'might prove to be a substantial help for our Russian allies'. Sixteen Lancasters were detailed for this raid from Upwood. One had to be withdrawn at the very start due to engine failure, while S/L Hague's aircraft developed engine trouble on the way to Chemnitz, and the starboard inner engine cut out. He reached the target on time, despite being on three engines, and landed back at Manston. Up in the north over the Yorkshire bases of the Canadian 6 Group, nine aircraft crashed very near their bases in freezing fog and icy conditions. Linton-on-Ouse suffered grievously in this way, losing three out of their fourteen Halifaxes on take-off with only one man surviving. One Halifax crashed in York bringing death to civilians, and a further twenty-two aircraft were lost on the operation. So near to the end of the war Chemnitz became a target of unhappy memory for the Canadian crews based in Yorkshire and for their grieving families.

On March 8th a new eastern target was attacked which contained important fighter production plants, the town of Dessau. The defences were alert and thirteen Lancasters, none from the sixteen proceeding from Upwood, were shot down. At first, in the ten tenths cloud, skymarkers were dropped, but, with the cloud gradually closing, a ground attack developed. That same night, in a 5 Group attack on the Harburg oil refinery 189 Squadron, based at Fulbeck, lost four out of the sixteen Lancasters sent out. Losses may have dropped, but there would be no 'milk runs'. A night attack on Hamburg on March 8/9th was directed against the U-boat docks, where a new type of U-boat was being assembled. This high quality U-boat would have given much trouble to allied convoys had it ever got off the assembly lines and into the oceans. S/L Clayton and F/L Harris controlled the raid. Illuminators placed their flares well, and exactly on time, so that the Aiming Point, with river, lake and docks, stood out clearly. The last night operation over Essen had taken place a short time ago. On March 11th it was the last daylight operation, with seven Upwood Lancasters acting as Blind Skymarkers and Visual Centerers. Although there was ten tenths cloud over the target this was an excellent *Wanganui* attack. The next day, March 12th, the same pair, as Master and Deputy, S/L Clayton and F/L Harris, controlled a daylight raid on Dortmund of 1,108 aircraft (a record), with a record tonnage of bombs, 4,851 tons, dropped, once again, through ten tenths cloud. On the night of March 13/14th four Upwood aircraft contributed their presence as Supporters for an attack on one of the few intact synthetic oil plants in the Gelsenkirchen region, Dahl Busch. A night attack on Homburg followed on March 14th, designed to deny passage to those German troops who would need to pass through the town to reinforce the crumbling front line.

On March 15th a night attack on the synthetic oil plant at Misburg near Hannover was directed by S/L Clayton as Master Bomber, and F/L Harris as Deputy. The next night an attack on Nuremberg (March 16/17th) saw many night fighters over the target. Some twenty-four Lancasters, all from 1 Group, were lost, most of them due to night fighters which mixed with the bomber stream over the target. Nor were the Pathfinders left alone. F/O Benson's Lancaster was attacked by a fighter on the bombing run. The gunners claimed that the attacker, an ME410, had been shot down. After their return to Upwood three wounded members of the crew had to be rushed to the R.A.F. Hospital in Ely. On the next night's operation, to Hanau, (March 18th) the fighters were up again, and waiting. F/L W. E. B. Mason was attacked by enemy aircraft after leaving the target, but evaded the fighters by corkscrewing. Another crew witnessed two JU88s leaving the target area, and saw three combats taking place. Even so, there were no 156 casualties and only one Lancaster was lost.

Over Heide, another synthetic oil plant, on the night of March 20th, the Master Bomber corrected the early bombing, which was very scattered. F/L Grant took off ten minutes after the others (fourteen other aircraft) from Upwood, and yet, even when the starboard inner engine became unserviceable, he managed to reach the target on time, to mark, and return to home base, another remarkable achievement. The only major Bomber Command raid of the war on Hildesheim took place during a deep daylight penetration into Germany on March 22nd. The railway links in Hildesheim join Berlin to the Rhine and the town contained important marshalling yards, as well as depots for troops. This raid is a classical example of the convergence of two kinds of bombing, the tactical and the strategic, with transport targets, troop interdictions and the old-style area attack all coming together.

On March 24th there was a daylight raid on Harpenweg, a synthetic oil plant near Dortmund, controlled by F/L T. S. Harris (Master Bomber) and F/L W. J. Cleland, D.F.C. (Deputy), with S/L P. F. Clayton, D.S.O., D.F.C. as Long Stop. There was good concentration in the bombing, with the Master Bomber keeping tight control of the raid. It was a small raid, with 173 Lancasters (of 1, 6 and 8 Group) and twelve Mosquitoes whose Oboe equipment enabled their T.Is to be so precisely dropped that the Master Bomber could mark visually. There were many explosions seen and all the evidence of a very successful raid.

An episode of incredible valour took place on this operation. F/O Hampson's aircraft, a 156 Lancaster from Upwood, was already on the bombing run. The aircraft received a direct hit in the bomb bays, and yet, miraculously, the bombs were not detonated, and some fell out of the shattered bomb bay. The flight engineer, Sgt. D. R. Bowers, had received a nasty thigh wound, and the Lancaster filled with smoke, and started to dive. The pilot gave the order to 'Bale out', although he continued to weave and take evasive action to avoid the predicted flak. After receiving the order to abandon, the first navigator and the wireless operator baled out. The rear gunner, F/S J. R. Mann, reported that the mid-upper gunner was missing, even though his parachute was still there in his turret. Underneath the mid-upper turret, however, a huge shell hole was discovered, and, since the aircraft was full of smoke, it was assumed (rightly, as it turned out) that he had fallen through this hole in the suffocating, near blinding conditions, during which the hole would not be seen.

It was at this point that the stricken Lancaster responded to the controls, and F/O Hampson cancelled the order to abandon. The set operator/second navigator, F/S F. G. Reynolds, was on the point of helping the wounded flight engineer to bale out. When the 'Bale out' order was cancelled, he called out to the rear gunner, F/S Mann, and both sought to help the badly wounded man back onto the flight deck inside the aircraft. Sgt. Bowers had, as has been explained, a thigh wound, with the splintered bone causing great pain. For all this, the flight engineer had continued to throw out 'Window' down the chute to confuse the radar-predicted flak guns.

Just as Sgt. Bowers was being dragged back again into the Lancaster, another direct hit from flak almost severed his left leg at the knee. When he had been carried to the flight deck beside the pilot, Sgt. Bowers, who had been a medical orderly, gave instructions over the dressing of his wound, and injected himself with morphia in the left wrist. In this gravely wounded state, the flight engineer still continued to give F/O Hampson advice about those things pertaining to his job. He commented on the state of the fuel tanks and gave instructions as to when they were to be changed, dragging his shattered body nearer to the switches. Meanwhile, the rear gunner, F/S Mann, helped the captain, and F/S Reynolds, the set operator, navigated back to Manston, where the aircraft was grounded as being 'Category E', that is, beyond repair. During the next month F/O Hampson was awarded an immediate D.F.C., F/S Mann and Reynolds were awarded immediate D.F.Ms, while Sgt. Bowers, the flight engineer, was awarded an immediate C.G.M.

That was a sticky night for a number of crews, even though 156 suffered no total crew casualties. S/L Clayton, the Long Stop, remained over the target while the raid was in progress to carry out his duties, and landed with so many holes in his Lancaster that it was placed in a very low category of serviceability.

A 'daylight' on Munster on March 25th saw some scattered bombing, although F/L Cleland, D.F.C., the Master Bomber, soon rectified the situation with his urgent and persistent instructions. The Deputy was F/L Deramore-Denver, an Australian pilot who had not been long at Upwood, but who was making a reputation for himself. On the last day of the month, March 31st, sixteen Upwood Lancasters joined in an attack by 469 aircraft on the Blohm and Voss shipyards in Hamburg. Once again, the object of the raid was to prevent the new and more powerful U-boat types from being assembled. The day fighters of the Luftwaffe made one of their last concerted assaults on the bomber force on this raid. Over the target the flak was heavy, it was predicted, and in barrage form. The new German jet fighters, ME262s were out over Hamburg, and there were several combats between them and 156 crews, with one ME262 claimed as damaged. Imagine, if you can, a Lancaster, with a full bomb load corkscrewing to evade a German jet. Eleven bombers, three of them Pathfinders, failed to return from this raid. Two of the three missing Pathfinders were Lancasters of 156 Squadron, captained by F/L A. C. Pope, D.F.C. and F/O H. Benson, D.F.C. It was a chastening experience for 156. They had taken the brunt of the terrific casualties in Wellingtons, and of the Ruhr and Berlin battles, and even now the 'Reaper', as aircrew described these events, personalising the fate which overtook many of their comrades, refused to leave them alone.

April started with two days of training flights. There had not been a lot of time for these during the first three months of 1945 with the multifarious tasks facing Pathfinders, and the fluctuating targets of various kinds. On April 3rd a frustrating day was experienced by all squadron personnel. Sixteen Lancasters were detailed for 'ops', only for these to be cancelled. Another sixteen Lancasters were detailed for a night raid, which was 'scrubbed' when they were bombed up, and ready, with the crews in them, waiting to be given the 'green'. Sixteen aircraft were again detailed for an early morning daylight raid, and, even while the crews were being briefed, at the traditionally impossible hour for early morning 'daylights', the 'op' was yet again, like the others, 'scrubbed'. You can imagine the strain on the armourers and ground crew. Bombing up and de-bombing had to be done carefully and precisely. Even with all the care and skill in the world, fatal accidents did happen, as has been demonstrated in the course of this narrative. Exhaustion set in after a twenty-four hour period like this. 'You just worked all the time, until the job was done,' Taff Jones recalled. Ground crew performed remarkable feats of endurance on occasions like these many, many times over in the course of the long war.

The next day, April 4th, Lancasters were made ready for night raids on two targets, Harburg, near Hamburg, and Lutzkendorf near Leipzig. The sixteen from Upwood were a part of a force of 1,172 bombers sent out that night to attack various targets, the majority of them to synthetic oil plants at the two locations attacked by Lancasters from 156 Squadron, and some to the oil plant at Leuna. It is interesting to note that 100 Group, the Group that dealt with Radio Counter Measures, and based near to the Norfolk coast, sent out 136 aircraft that night. On April 7th the 'op' for sixteen Lancasters was scrubbed, and the Squadron Navigator Leader, S/L R. H. Dean, D.F.C., who was also the H2S Leader, was posted to the N.T.U. at Warboys. With the end of the war in sight there was no suspension of normal procedures. A section leader was screened, and moved to where he was most needed. And that same day, coming in the opposite direction, from the N.T.U. at Warboys to 156 at Upwood for operational duties, arrived two pilots, F/O A. G. Edgar, D.F.C., and F/O D. A. Millikin, D.F.C. It was business as usual, whatever expectations there were in the air.

The Blohm and Voss works at Hamburg were revisited yet again on April 3rd, the last major raid of the war, with ten Upwood Lancasters taking part, while Kiel was attacked on the next night (April 9th), with sixteen Lancasters from Upwood contributing. Two Master Bombers and two Deputies controlled this complicated raid on two aiming points. U-boat yards were severely damaged, the *Admiral Scheer*, a pocket battleship, was hit and capsized, the *Admiral Hipper* and the *Emden* were damaged and crippled. 'Should be a very highly successful raid,' the entry in the *Operations Record Book* of 156 comments, as indeed it was. On April 10th a daylight attack took place on the Engelsdorf and Mackau railway marshalling yards at Leipzig, with the squadron supplying four Lancasters. Nine other Lancasters of 156 took part that night in an attack on Plauen south of Leipzig. S/L K. H. Letford, D.S.O., D.F.C. was Master Bomber on this raid, while F/L Deramore-Denver was his Deputy. S/L Letford had been with the squadron since the earlier months of 1944. He captained a much decorated crew, with a first navigator who had a D.F.C. and Bar, F/L T. Kennedy, who rejoiced in the nickname of 'Tiger' Kennedy. On the day of these two raids, April 10th, the squadron received a new C.O. W/C A. J. L. Craig, D.S.O., D.F.C. took over command in succesion to W/C T. E. Ison. D.S.O., D.F.C., the tall and well-built Master Bomber, whom everyone, ground crew included, called 'Tiny'. He was posted away to No. 7. Group.

A 'daylight' to Nuremberg on April 11th saw F/L Wallace, as Primary Visual Marker, identify the Aiming Point clearly, and with great precision, with huge explosions observed in the marshalling yards which were the object of the attack. F/L Wallace, D.F.C., was tragically killed in a flying accident in India after the war. Bill Davies, the second navigator or set operator, in F/L Wallace's crew, writes about the 'ops' completed by this crew in the last seven months of the war, with the rear gunner Sgt. James Hayton thought to be a 'grandfather figure' at thirty-five or thirty-six years old. You can read F/L Davies' remarks on these hectic final months at Upwood in Chaz Bowyer's *Pathfinders at War*, published by Ian Allan Ltd in 1977. Kiel was attacked in a night raid on April 13th, and an attack on Potsdam followed, also by night, on April 14th. On this raid fifteen Upwood Lancasters took off, with a reserve crew having to be included in that number. The pilot of this crew, F/L W. J. Taylor, encountered a packet of troubles. When he was about sixty miles from the target, his port outer engine cut out, the rear turret became u/s, with the mid-upper turret partially u/s, Despite all this, F/L Taylor pressed on, arrived three minutes late over the target, and made a successful bombing run from 14,000 feet.

On the night of April 16th fifteen Lancasters from Upwood attacked the railway marshalling yards at Schwandorf, with S/L Clayton as Master Bomber, and F/L James as Deputy. The raid began with a scattering of flares but later a concentrated pattern emerged, covering the aiming point. One Lancaster did not get back to Upwood from this raid, the only aircraft lost on this night from the 167 Lancasters and eight Mosquitoes of the force attacking Schwandorf. About this missing aircraft (Lancaster PB625) it is worth giving details in full, as the entire crew, all of whom were killed, were the last operational aircrew casualties of the war in 156 Squadron. They were as follows:

F/O J. Jamieson Pilot

F/O F. W. O'Reilly First navigator

F/S D. E. Smith W/Op

Sgt. F. J. Cuthill F/E

P/O F. L. Ponting Second navigator

P/O H. W. Elliot (Canadian) M/U/G

Sgt. E. Wilson R/G

They were on the squadron for just over three weeks, having been posted from the N.T.U. at Warboys on March 21st, after serving on 625 Squadron at Kelstern in Lincolnshire. To go down like this, twenty days before the cessation of hostilities, was hard for the families of the missing men and for their colleagues on 156 Squadron.

Heligoland, Manna and Exodus

On April 18th 969 aircraft raided by day the naval base, airfield and town on Heligoland. Eight aircraft took off from Upwood and 156 provided the controller for this classic raid, F/L T. S. Harris as Master Bomber, and the C.O., W/C Craig, as Deputy Master Bomber. Photographs of the target area, often reproduced in the literature of Bomber Command, show the entire area and island as something resembling a lunar landscape. Three Halifaxes from 4 Group were lost on this raid. A 'daylight' on Bremen on April 22nd saw a flurry of activity within 156 Squadron. Fourteen Lancasters were dispatched, the Master Bomber was F/L T. S. Harris, with W/C R. F. Griffin, D.S.O., D.F.C. as Deputy. As Long Stop, were S/L K. H. Letford, D.S.O., D.F.C. and S/L P. F. Clayton, D.S.O., D.F.C. This raid was a preparation for the assault on Bremen about to be made by the British advancing XXX Corps. In view of the proximity of our own troops, F/L Harris, the Master Bomber, aborted the mission. On April 25th the last operational bombing raid of 156 Squadron took place, when sixteen Lancasters joined in a daylight attack by 482 aircraft on Wangerooge, an island in the Frisians which controlled the water routes to Bremen and Wilhelmshaven. Once more, 156 Squadron provided the experts to control this highly successful raid, with S/L A. W. G. Cochrane, D.S.O., D.F.C. and 2 Bars as Master Bomber, and F/L H. G. Hughes as Deputy. Seven aircraft (five Halifaxes and two Lancasters, none from 156) were lost, with six out of seven being involved in collisions, and losing thereby twenty-eight Canadians and thirteen British aircrew. The seventh aircraft which was lost was from 347 Squadron, the Free French Squadron stationed at Elvington near York, now the home of the Yorkshire Aviation Museum.

A very different kind of operation took place on April 30th, when eight Lancasters of the squadron flew by day to Rotterdam to mark areas where food supplies might be dropped to a starving Dutch population. Pathfinders released their T.Is over a huge white cross laid out on the ground. Parcels of food were then dropped on the markers. Some burst on impact, others did not. A nearby house was accidentally set on fire. None of this, however, stopped the local population from expressing their enthusiasm in a spontaneous, demonstrative way. People went wild when they saw the Lancasters coming in, waving flags, tablecloths, anything they could find. Further drops of food were carried out early the following month, on Rotterdam on May 2nd, when the crews discovered that the white cross was, by now, not as white as before, and was hence difficult to identify, and at the Hague on May 3rd, where 156 crews saw the words 'TABAC S.V.P.' painted on a house. Tobacco was obviously as scarce as was food to the local Dutch population. On May 5th another drop on Rotterdam took place. As the cross was by now something resembling a grey colour, only four of the seven aircraft who took off for Rotterdam from Upwood dropped their T.Is over it. So ended a series of welcome 'ops', code-named *Operation Manna*.

Operation Exodus, the bringing back of liberated P.O.Ws, was to follow. On May 7th ten Lancasters of the squadron flew to an aerodrome near Brussels to bring back those P.O.Ws recently liberated to specially designated reception points. Those first P.O.Ws were brought back to Westcott in Buckinghamshire, 240 of them, as were 240 the next day, who were delivered to Wing, another Buckinghamshire aerodrome.

On this next day, however, May 8th, 1945, the news was broadcast of the surrender of the German armed forces. V.E. Day, so long awaited, was here. At

3.00pm in the afternoon the Prime Minister made the official declaration, while H. M. the King spoke in a radio broadcast at 9.00pm. Before this, at 10.00am that morning, the squadron formed part of a Station Thanksgiving Parade 'dedicated to the cessation of hostilities in Europe'. The entry in the *Operations Record Book* of 156 Squadron has a sober reflection after this:

'And so ends the Squadron's contribution to air warfare in the European War, during which the Squadron lost 913 gallant comrades. Fortunately 86 are P.O.W., and 25 have since returned to their country.'

That very day, as has already been recorded, ten 156 aircraft took off on another 'Exodus' operation. On the next day, May 9th, eight Lancasters from Upwood flew to Lubeck, bringing back 192 P.O.Ws to Wing, with A/V/M/ Bennett piloting one of the Lancasters. On May 10th eight more Lancasters took off for Lubeck and returned to Seighford in Staffordshire with 118 more P.O.Ws, British and American, army and air force. From May 15th onwards Upwood aircraft switched to Juvencourt as a collecting point for P.O.Ws, bringing back 360 to Wing on that day, with the benefit of superb prior organisation set in motion by Upwood's Station Commander G/C S. W. B. Menaul, D.F.C., A.F.C., who flew in one of the 156 aircraft to inspect suitable airfields and points of assembly. Juvencourt was used again in two full operations to airlift P.O.Ws on May 23rd and 24th. On May 26th eight 156 aircraft approaching Juvencourt to collect P.O.Ws were recalled just as they drew up to the assembly point. One Lancaster of the squadron, despite this, landed and returned with twenty-four P.O.Ws from the Greek army.

On May 22nd there began a series of flights popularly called – and it did become the official name – 'Cook's Tours' over devastated areas of Germany. On May 22nd the first of these flights took place (three Lancasters taking eighteen ground staff over the Ruhr), on the 23rd three aircraft took thirteen ground personnel on another Cook's Tour, while on the same day two Upwood Lancasters flew back to Juvencourt, one of them bringing twenty-four P.O.Ws back. The second Lancaster flying to Juvencourt was piloted by G/C Menaul, with A/V/M/ J. B. Whitley, D.S.O., A.F.C. as second pilot. The next day, May 24th, saw the last day for 156 to play a part in *Operation Exodus*, with ten Lancasters bringing back 241 men from Juvencourt to Dunsfold. Operations to take ground staff and other personnel to see for themselves the effects of the bombing lasted throught May and into June. Additional flights were also made to Nuremberg to bring back battle weary soldiers for a well-earned leave. On June 27th it was goodbye to Upwood and a move to Wyton where the squadron was disbanded on September 25th. As the *Operations Record Book* remarks, in closing, on that day: 'We no longer ''Light the Way''.'

F/S Philip Wadsworth (second from left with some other members of the crew at Elsham Wolds.
(Taff Jones)

Bottom left F/S Philip Wadsworth at Elsham Wolds out on the dispersal.
(Taff Jones)

Bottom F/O Philip Wadsworth with the author, taken on his last leave.
(Mrs. Margaret Wadsworth)

CHAPTER 8

ENDINGS

'To what purpose is this waste?'

(Matthew. 26:8)

When the dust of war had settled, what a cost there was, seventeen Wellingtons lost during the Pathfinder period of 156 Squadron, from August to December 1942 at Warboys, and 104 Lancasters lost during the rest of the time from Warboys and Upwood. If you go back to the period when 156 Squadron was at Alconbury, and in 3 Group from February 14th, 1942, up to the time of the move to Warboys, then you must add a further twenty-two missing Wellingtons to the tally of costs, 143 aircraft in all, 121 of them in 8 Group and in Pathfinders. The squadron's losses were exceptionally heavy during the Wellington period, and yet within Pathfinder heavy bomber squadrons 156 flew more sorties than any other Pathfinder squadron, and the most Lancaster sorties in 8 Group. The Pathfinder station at Oakington tops the number of missing aircraft (Stirlings and Lancasters, in the case of 7 Squadron) with a figure of 124 as compared with 121 for Warboys and Upwood. During the period of the Battle of Berlin, however, those dark days at Warboys and Upwood, the squadron suffered more casualties than any other Pathfinder squadron, 168 men killed, with eleven as P.O.Ws, in comparison with 7 Squadron's 146 men killed, and thirty-nine P.O.Ws.

In my view Bomber Command's contribution, and within it the contribution of the Pathfinders, and within their midst, the contribution made by 156 Squadron, was incalculable. Perhaps I can do no better thing than to repeat here, at the end of this chronicle, a sermon (very lightly revised) I preached at the parish church of Warboys, the church of St. Mary Magdalene, which resounded to the thunder of those aircraft all those years ago. For the sermon, preached on May 13th, 1990, seeks to answer some of the questions subsequent generations have asked of the bomber offensive, in which the Pathfinders led the way for the bombers on hazardous raid after raid. St. Mary Magdalene, where the sermon was preached, remembers the Pathfinders: hymn boards are dedicated in their honour, a notice board stands outside the church, as well as lych gates, and conifers planted outside, all donated by the Pathfinder Association, not to mention the beautiful memorial window, dedicated in May 1991.

For me those men I have met at the reunions, and those lost comrades of 156 Squadron, some of whom figure in the pages of this chronicle, remain eternally young, and, approaching the fiftieth anniversary of the foundation of the Pathfinder force, it seemed right and appropriate to tell their story. I had not anticipated so many tales of heroism within our Squadron's story, nor had I realised that so many young men of aircrew kept the faith, as it were, to the very end, to the inevitable end, as I did when I went, two years ago, in search of a flight engineer.

To What Purpose is this Waste?

Jesus was asked this question by disciples when a woman made a costly act of devotion to him (Matthew 26 : 6-13). You remember that in the story Jesus was having supper at the house of a very proper, socially conscious Pharisee. A woman of ill repute came in from the street and poured an alabaster jar of very precious ointment all over Jesus' feet and head. Even his friends were scandalised. 'To what purpose,' they said, 'is this waste? The ointment could have been sold to provide support for the poor. This is sheer prodigal waste!'

Over the past four decades and longer many have been asking the same question, 'To what purpose is this waste?' Only this time they have been asking it of the sacrifices made by your friends and contemporaries and colleagues. Why, to what purpose is this loss of life? For what a reckoning, what a cost there was: 55,573 killed in Bomber Command forces as a whole, including 1,570 ground crew, and in the Pathfinder force alone, between its formation in August 1942 and the end of the war, 3,618 dead. My father, joining 156 on his second tour as a flight engineer, perished in the crew of one of the C.Os of 156 Squadron, Group Captain Eaton, in April 1944 over Friedrichshafen.

So, even though I was a mere ten months old when my father died, and even though I am over twice his age now, I have a personal interest in asking this question – to what purpose is this waste?

I was born and grew up in a little East Riding town not unconnected with the bomber offensive – Driffield in East Yorkshire. As a clergyman I have worked half of my ministry in academic life, and half in the very different surroundings of three Northern Rugby League towns, before recently moving to a parish not very far from here. Over the time I have often sought to interpret this question 'to what purpose?' to the young of a different generation, to students and younger enquirers, who are quite quick to point out to me the rights and wrongs of bombing, without having an inkling of the depths of Naziism or having any appreciation of the need – the morally absolute need – to wage war with every weapon at our disposal, to defeat Hitler, and to make the world free enough for the students of our western and eastern democracies to make their protests in, if they wish. The spectacle of the death camps, of genocide, the sufferings of the Jewish teachers and lecturers, who influenced me and taught me over the years must be an answer to the question – to what purpose? For the supreme immorality in my belief (and I have joined this debate with many audiences in the past and have become a kind of tame cleric to be wheeled in when these things are debated), the supreme immorality in my belief was not to press the war against Hitler with every means at our disposal, not to make it in such a way that it brought a speedy and successful conclusion. The great immorality, by any set of canons, was not to press it relentlessly, and area-wide, and therefore to postpone the re-establishment of a just and merciful world order. As your then leader Sir Arthur Harris of Bomber Command said at the start of it all, quoting the prophet Hosea in a rather robust phrase: 'They have sown the wind, and they shall reap the whirlwind.' Out of the whirlwind comes the peace. To what purpose – to what purpose is this waste?

Let us turn from the attitudes of later generations to you forty-five years ago and more, doing a job night after night, several nights a week, sometimes, as during the Battle of Berlin, several consecutive nights a week, flying from these airfields not knowing if you would return, watching the odds mount against you. There's a wonderful passage in one of the first books to have been published about the Pathfinders. The book was called simply *Pathfinders* and was written in 1946 by Wing Commander William Anderson, and he writes, and I quote: 'Aircrew were not saints, even less so than most men, but like all men they had inside them a longing for better things.' It is this longing, this longing for better things that you had, when you did this job. 'Aircrew were not saints,' says Wing Commander Anderson, but then there is an awful lot of nonsense talked about saints, who, in my understanding, are really sinners who go on trying. Aircrew were not perfect – and now another story about this. A vicar stood up and said to his congregation, 'Stand up those who are perfect.' Nobody stood up. Nobody stood up (I tried that this morning – nobody stood up). He said again, 'Stand up those who are perfect,' and again no one stood up. A third time he said, 'Stand up those who are perfect,' and his church warden stood up. He said, 'I didn't know you were perfect, Jack.' He replied, 'I'm not, but I'm standing up to represent my wife's first husband!'

You went out and you did what you did. You went on trying, and you kept your morale, led by Air Vice Marshal Bennett, to whom morale was of the essence, through some very tough, very bleak times!

Let's go back to the story in the gospel about the woman who spent all she had on an alabaster jar of precious ointment and who prompted that question - To what purpose is this waste?

Jesus rebuked those who asked the question and ended by saying, 'Wherever this gospel is preached in the whole world, what she has done will be told in memory of her.'

For we are here this morning to remember, to recall those who went through the furnace, and, in the words of the laconic entry at the end of the log book, 'failed to return', and to give thanks for our past and present deliverances. And so, taking up the words of this gospel story, wherever and whenever the great struggle for freedom, that last great conflict which has shaped our world and our lives is talked about, what you, the Pathfinders, have done, will be told as a memorial. You are Pathfinders – you found the way, marked the target, and I believe that you have shown to future generations a way, a way which points out what young men and young women (for let's not forget the W.A.A.Fs, the wives, the widows) can do and suffer for what they believe in, can do because of their high morale and longing for better things.

We need now more than ever before, as you are growing older, we need now to talk about you, and to remember you, and not to forget you, as we seek a way, a way like you did, through a similarly dark world, into the next millenium. So let us remember, let us give thanks, and for God's sake even though I know you are not perfect, let us never ever lose this longing for better things.

I'll close with a poem, a short poem by John Pudney which I dare say you have heard before. It's about you, leaving to go on yet another one of those raids one of those nights forty-five, forty-six, forty-seven, forty-eight years ago – and I'll close with this:

> 'Empty your pockets, Tom, Dick and Harry,
> Strip your identity; leave it behind.
> Lawyer, garage hand, grocer, don't tarry
> With your own country, with your own kind.
>
> 'Leave all your letters. Suburb and township,
> Green fen and grocery, slipway and bay,
> Hot springs and prairie, smokestack and coal tip,
> Leave in our keeping while you're away.
>
> 'Tom, Dick and Harry, plain names and numbers,
> Pilot, observer, and gunner depart.
> Their personal litter only encumbers
> Somebody's head, somebody's heart.'

Amen.

APPENDIX

Letters received by the author's mother on 28th April, 1944., and 6th October, 1944.

No. 156 Squadron,
Royal Air Force,
Upwood, Hunts.
28th April, 1944.

Dear Mrs. Wadsworth,

It is with deep regret that I write to confirm the sad news which you have already received regarding your husband, Pilot Officer P. Wadsworth.

His aircraft was engaged in an attack on Friedrichshaven on the night of the 27/28th April, 1944, but as no message was received from the aircraft there is little that can be added to the bare statement reporting him as 'Missing'.

Pilot Officer Wadsworth was a member of an outstanding crew, and I am sure that he and his companions gave a very good account of themselves. I can only hope that they were able to make a safe landing either by parachute or in the aircraft itself.

News of this nature, however, reaches us only through the International Red Cross Committee, and normally takes up to six weeks to come through. My sympathy, and that of all members of my squadron is with you in this anxious time of waiting.

It is desired to explain that the request in the telegram notifying you of the casualty to your husband was included with the object of avoiding his chance of escape being prejudiced by undue publicity in case he was still at large. This is not to say that any information about him is available, but is a precaution adopted in the case of all personnel reported missing.

Please be assured that any information received will be communicated to you immediately, and do not hesitate to write if I can be of any service.

Yours Sincerely,

T.W.G. GODFREY (Signed)

Squadron Leader, Commanding
No. 156 Squadron, R.A.F.

AIR MINISTRY
(Casualty Branch)
73, OXFORD STREET,
W1.
6th October, 1944.

Madam,

I am directed to refer to the letter dated the 4th May, 1944, from this Department, notifying you that your husband, Flying Officer P. Wadsworth, Royal Air Force, was reported missing as a result of air operations on the night of 27th/28th April, 1944, and to inform you, with regret, that although no definite news of him has come to hand, telegraphic reports have been received from the International Red Cross Committee.

Unfortunately in these reports the German Authorities have mixed the occupants of two aircraft which were missing as a result of an attack on Friedrichshaven on the night of 27th/28th. April, 1944.

The crews of these aircraft were:-

1) Acting Group Captain E.C. Eaton D.F.C.,
   Acting Squadron Leader L.H. Glasspool, D.F.C.,
   Flying Officer Franklin
   Flying Officer J.R. Dodds
   Flying Officer P. Wadsworth
   Flight Lieutenant C.A. Kidd
   Flying Officer R.G. Sharland D.F.C.

2) Flying Officer R.W. Herron
   Flight Sergeant M.R. Henderson
   Sergeant W.R. Percival
   Flying Officer E.W. McLachlan
   Sergeant J.W. Germing
   Warrant Officer K.A. Smith
   Flying Officer P.E. Chilman

In the first reports from the German Authorities it was stated that Flying Officer J.R. Dodds, Flying Officer K.G. Franklin, Flying Officer R.G. Sharland D.F.C., Flight Lieutenant C.A. Kidd of Crew No 1, and Warrant Officer K.A. Smith of Crew No. 2 lost their lives on 28th April, 1944.

A further report states that Sergeant W.R. Percival of Crew No. 2, 'Sergeant Ward', and three members whose identity the German Authorities are unable to establish at present, also lost their lives on 28th April, 1944.

Sergeant Ward, who was not a member of either of these crews, was captured from a later operation on 21st May, 1944. It is thought that a member of your husband's crew was in possession of effects bearing the name of 'Ward', who belonged to the same Squadron, and was thus erroneously identified by the German Authorities as 'Ward'.

As there were fourteen members in two crews, it will be appreciated that it is not possible on present information to state precisely who are the three unidentified members, or the airman referred to as 'Ward'. It is hoped, however, that when the confirmatory German official death lists are received the position will be clarified.

Meanwhile, I am to express the Air Ministry's sympathy with you in your grave anxiety, and to assure you that you will be at once informed of any further news which may be received.

I am, Madam,
Your obedient Servant,

M. Gray. (Signed)

For Director of Personal Services.

An exchange of memories. From left to right; G/C H. R. Hall, O.B.E., D.F.C., Mrs Diana Sewerby, Taff Jones, Mrs Ly Bennett, A/V/M P. M. S. Hedgeland, C.B., O.B.E., and P. E. C. L. Richard, D.F.C. (Taff Jones)

The new Upwood memorial tablet. *(Taff Jones)*

The new memorial window in St. Mary Magdalene Church, Warboys, dedicated in May, 1991, to the Pathfinders.

(Taff Jones)

The new Warboys memorial tablet.

(Taff Jones)

W/C Womersley, D.S.O., D.F.C., and crew (with the Squadron Signals Leader F/L Cook, D.F.C. on his left). (Taff Jones)

Lancaster R for Robert flying over Warboys airfield, with church of St. Mary Magdalene in the background (from an original painting). (Taff Jones)

BIBLIOGRAPHY

A) Published Works

W/C W. Anderson, OBE, DFC, AFC: *Pathfinders* (Jarrolds 1946).

R. Barker: *The Thousand Plan.*(Chatto and Windus, 1965).

A/V/M/ D.C.T. Bennett: *Pathfinder* (Frederick Muller 1958).

Chaz Bowyer: *Path Finders at War* (Ian Allan 1977).

M.J.F. Bowyer: *Action stations 1. Wartime Military Airfields of East Anglia 1939 - 1945* (Patrick Stephens 1979).

A. Brookes: *Bomber Squadron at War* (Ian Allan 1983).

J. Campbell: *The Bombing of Nuremberg* (Allison & Busby 1973).

D. E. Charlwood: *No Moon Tonight* (Angus and Robertson 1956).

W.R. Chorley: *In Brave Company: 158 Squadron Operations* (P.A. Chorley, Salisbury 1990 2nd ed).

P.G. Cooksley *Wellington: Mainstay of Bomber Command* (Patrick Stephens 1987).

A.W. Cooper: *Bombers over Berlin* (William Kimber 1985).

A.G. Goulding: *Uncommon Valour* (Merlin Books, Braunton 1983).

J.F. Hamlin: *The Royal Air Force in Cambridgeshire Part 4: The Histories of RAF Upwood and RAF Warboys* (John F. Hamlin 1990).

M. Hastings: *Bomber Command* (Michael Joseph 1979).

S.B. Hazard & G/C D.F.E.C. Deane: *They're Not Shooting at You Now, Grandad* (S.B. Hazzard 1991).

E. Hazelhoff: *Soldier of Orange* (Hodder & Stoughton 1972).

A.S. Jackson: *Pathfinder Bennett, Airman Extraordinary* (Terence Dalton Ltd., Lavenham 1991).

N. Longmate: *The Bombers: The RAF Offensive Against Germany 1939 - 1945* (Hutchinson 1983).

G/C T.G.Mahaddie, DSO, DFC, AFC, CZMC, CENG, FRAeS: *Hamish* (Ian Allan 1989).

F.K Mason: *The Avro Lancaster* (Aston Publications 1989).

M. Middlebrook: *The Nuremberg Raid* (Penguin, Harmondsworth 1973, 2nd ed. 1980).

M. Middlebrook: *The Battle of Hamburg* (Penguin Harmondsworth 1980).

M. Middlebrook: *The Peenemunde Raid* (Penguin Harmondsworth 1982).

M. Middlebrook: *The Berlin Raids* (Penguin Harmondsworth 1988).

M. Middlebrook & C. Everitt: *The Bomber Command War Diaries: An Operational Reference Book 1939 - 1945* (Viking 1985).

P.J.R. Moyes: *Bomber Squadrons of the RAF and Their Aircraft* (Macdonald 1964).

G. Musgrove: *Pathfinder Force. A History of 8 Group* (Macdonald & Jane's, 1976).

P. Ryle: *Missing in Action: May - September 1944* (W.H Allen 1979).

A/C J.Searby, DSO, DFC: *The Everlasting Arms* (William Kimber 1988).

A/C J.Searby, DSO, DFC: T*he Bomber Battle for Berlin* (Airlife Pubishing 1991).

R. Smith: *Rear Gunner Pathfinders* (Goodall Publications 1987).

G. Taylor: *The Nuremberg Massacre* (Sidgwick & Jackson 1980).

Sir Charles Webster & N. Frankland, DFC.: *The Strategic Air Offensive Against Germany 1939 - 1945* (London HMSO 1961).

Dr. R. Winfield DFC, AFC: *The Sky Belongs to Them* (William Kimber 1976).

S/L W. G. Manifold, D.F.C. and Bar: *Never a Dull!* (Camperdown, Victoria, Australia 1986.).

R. S. Nielsen: *With the Stars Above* (Olympia, Washington 1984).

Novels

H.E. Bates: T*he Stories of Flying Officer X* (Jonathan Cape 1952).

W. Clapham: *Night be My Witness* (Jonathan Cape 1952).

W. Coyle: *Act of Grace* (Chatto & Windus 1988).

L. Deighton: *Bomber* (Jonathan Cape 1970).

Spencer Dunmore: *Bomb Run* (Peter Davies 1971).

H.J. Wright: *Pathfinders 'Light the Way'* (McCann Publishing, Brisbane 1983).

B) Primary Sources

The Operational Records Book of 156 Squadron is deposited in the Public Records Office, Kew, with a microfilm copy available in the County Record Office, Shire Hall, Cambridge.

The reference number of the ORB is *AIR 1041*

I have also consulted *log books and diaries* especially the log books of my father, and of Ron Breeze, and Ron Breeze's valuable and lengthy diary.

The unpublished memoirs of G/C H. R. Hall, O.B.E., D.F.C., *Time Flying*, have been of the greatest help.

I am deeply indebted to the work compiled by F/L R. Trotter, DFC: *The 156 Squadron Register of Members of the Royal Air Force Alconbury, Warboys, Upwood, and Wyton 1942 - 1945*, with its interesting and informative notes. It was completed after November 1st, 1991, with 172 members' entries and updated on January 1st 1992 with a brief Supplement bringing the number of entries to 181.